Hendrickson

PREACHING ON THE LORD'S SUPPER
Encounter with Christ

IAN MacLEOD

HENDRICKSON
PUBLISHERS
PEABODY, MASSACHUSETTS 01961-3473

First published 1990 by Mowbray, a Cassell imprint, London

PREACHING ON THE LORD'S SUPPER:
ENCOUNTER WITH CHRIST

© Ian MacLeod 1990

Hendrickson Publishers, Inc., Edition 1994

ISBN 1-56563-047-5

Reprinted by arrangement with Mowbray,
an imprint of Cassell plc, London.

Printed in the United States of America

CONTENTS

ACKNOWLEDGEMENTS

The author gratefully acknowledges: the Salvationist Publishing and Supplies Ltd, London, for permission to quote a stanza from Albert Orsborn's hymn 'My life must be Christ's broken bread' © Salvationist Publishing and Supplies Ltd; Gill and Macmillan Ltd, Dublin, for permission to reproduce the poem 'The Brick', from *Prayers of Life* by Michel Quoist; The Society of Authors, as the literary representative of the Estate of John Masefield, for permission to quote an extract from 'The Everlasting Mercy'; Hodder and Stoughton for permission to quote John Donne's 'A Hymne to God the Father' from *An Outline of Religion For Children*, by E. R. Appleton; The Diocese of Westminster for permission to quote two stanzas from Sister M. Xavier's hymn 'Lord, for tomorrow and its needs'; the *Daily Express* for permission to quote part of the 'Lament for James, Earl of Glencairn' by Robert Burns, from the Kilmarnock Edition of the *Poetical Works of Robert Burns*, published in a special edition by the Scottish Daily Express, Glasgow, 1938.

Every effort has been made to trace the sources of all copyright material, and if any unwitting infringement has occurred, we offer our apologies and would appreciate notification.

FOREWORD

For ministers like myself who have found the preparation of their sermons for those occasions when the sacrament of Holy Communion was being celebrated particularly difficult, who have found it hard to find thoughts and words which might more adequately serve to illuminate the sacrament for their people, this collection of sermons should prove a treasure house to which they may return with profit again and again. The sermons are all uncompromisingly biblical in their approach and message, and often shed a fresh light on some of our familiar Communion hymns. At the same time they are not lacking in contemporary illustrations and modern and literary references. I could have wished, when I was in the active ministry, to have had them by me. My preaching on those sacramental occasions might have been more useful to my people.

E. G. BALLS. MA, BD, STM, DD

TO NANCY

My wife, friend and constant companion

PREFACE

In the Church of Scotland, the sacrament of the Lord's Supper is, by
and large, celebrated infrequently. This was not the desire of the
Reformers. Calvin believed in a weekly celebration, and only for the
sake of peace with the burghers of Geneva, accepted a less frequent
observance 'for the time being', while Knox, in the Book of Common
Order, intended it to be celebrated on a monthly basis. Nevertheless,
a tradition, however it originates, is difficult to alter, and numerous
attemps to introduce a more frequent celebration on a wide scale have
proved unsuccessful. The quarterly celebration in towns and the
biannual celebration in rural areas, therefore, still tends to be the
prevailing pattern.

While that situation may not be desirable, it does mean that the
'Communion season' stands out as a particularly important occasion,
and its observance is spared the dullness of custom and routine. This
places a particular burden on the preacher, whose joy and pain it is on
these occasions to dwell on the most holy things of the faith, and in
his preaching to point those who gather to celebrate to the One whose
sacrifice made once and for all on our behalf is represented vividly in
the Holy Supper.

These addresses are offered by one to whom words do not come
easily. They are the sermons of an ordinary preacher, not of a scholar,
but it is to be hoped that the reader will not find them wanting in
taking account of the invaluable help which the scholars render in
exegetical comment. All were preached to the congregations of
Brodick and Corrie on the island of Arran, and they are offered more
widely, in the hope that they may stimulate ideas for others in their
preaching at the Lord's Supper, or to the casual reader, in furthering
an understanding of its significance.

Four of the addresses have already appeared in the *Expository
Times*: 'The Three Perspectives of the Lord's Supper', August 1976,
p. 337: 'Enough and to Spare', January 1977, p. 114: 'The Night of

Betrayal', July 1981, p. 312: 'All Encompassing Love', July 1986, p. 306. All are reprinted here, more or less as they were edited to conform to the sermon length required by that publication, and I thank the editor for permission to reprint them.

I wish to record personal thanks to my Presbytery Clerk and kind friend, the Revd Dr George Balls, for reading the script and for helpful suggestions and advice.

I. M.

ENCOUNTER WITH CHRIST

(The sermon was preached with two large-size visual aids, miniatures of which are found inserted in the text below, at the relevant stages of the address.)

'What do you mean by this service?' EXODUS 12.26 (RSV)
'This is my body which is given for you.' LUKE 22.19 (RSV)

I wonder if you have ever heard the name of Wolfgang Köhler? Wolfgang Köhler was a psychologist of the Gestalt school, who, born in Estonia in the late nineteenth century, left his professor's chair in Berlin in 1935, in protest at the activities of the Nazi regime, and emigrated to America where he died about twenty years ago.

Now we are not here this morning, obviously, for a lecture in psychology, even were I competent to deliver one, which I am not. But I do want to show you, for the purpose of this sermon, one of the drawings of Wolfgang Köhler.

Wolfgang Köhler was interested in perception, which was the great concern of the Gestalt school. That is to say that he was interested in the way in which animals or human beings come to perceive things, the way in which we respond to stimuli to the senses.

Here is one of the drawings of Wolfgang Köhler, and it is known as the Köhler cross:

1

Now the interesting thing about the drawing is that, when you look at it, you should see a cross. But the question is, which cross do you see? I mean, look at it one way, and you can see very plainly a white cross, a cross in the shape of a Maltese cross, standing out against a black background.

But look at it another way. Stare at it long and hard enough, and the white cross should fade out. Then you will see a black cross, in the shape of a St Andrew cross, and it stands against a background which is white.

The point that Köhler was making with that drawing, is that we experience fluctuations of perception, or if you like, shifting perceptions, whenever the setting or background which stimulates our perception is not clearly defined.

That is the problem with this picture which I am displaying here. If the background to the picture is black, then what you see in the picture itself is a white Maltese cross. But if the background to the picture is white, then what you see in the picture is the cross of St Andrew in black.

Let me show you another drawing in which we experience the same thing, because I want to use this second drawing to illustrate the point of the sermon.

Here is a picture of a communion cup. Or, is it?

I mean, we have the same problem with this picture as we had with the other. The background to the picture is not clearly defined, so that we just do not know whether it is black or white. And the result is that, when we look at it, we experience shifting perceptions.

Look at it one way, and it is quite clearly a cup. What you see is a white goblet, standing out against a black background. But look at it another way. Look at it long and hard. And you should find that the white Communion cup will fade out, so that you will be able to see two black faces against a white background, the eyes, noses, mouths and chins pointing quite distinctly to their opposites.

Now just for the moment let's forget about Wolfgang Köhler and the lesson in perception. But, if you can, hold on in your mind to that second picture, because I think it can illustrate two different responses to this sacrament, which we come here to celebrate in church this morning.

1 I think there are those who come to the Lord's table, and all they can see in it, as it were, is the cup. What I mean is that, for some people who come to the sacrament, all they can see is a ritual. A ritual which involves the use of physical elements of bread and wine, and a ritual in which we indulge as Presbyterians three or four times in the year, though other denominations, for very good reasons, do it far more frequently.

Oh, it may be a little different from what happens on the normal Sunday. Especially as we come to the table service, where the bread is broken and the wine is shared, and special words are used which are always used at this service, and everyone in the congregation has the opportunity to take part. But, in the end of the day, ritual is what it is all about. It is about a ritual action, performed more or less according to a pattern, a ritual which the Church has perpetuated from the time of Christ, and a ritual which we believe originated from him, because it spoke of his death.

That is not to despise ritual, of course. Ritual actions and words play a very large part in all our lives. Far more, I think, that we sometimes realize. And without them something of life's pleasantry would disappear. The shake of a hand when we meet, the wave of an arm in recognition, the expression 'Goodbye' when we part – all of these are ritual expressions.

But there is a real weakness to such words and actions. And the weakness is that they can mean everything, or nothing. A shake of the hand can mean a genuine offer of friendship, or simply that we are doing the expected thing. A wave of the arm can convey the impression that somebody is really pleased to see us. But it could also be the case that they are happy to be on the other side of the street, and not required to stop and talk. And a goodbye may mean a sincere, 'God be with you', which is, of course, what the phrase really means, even in its contracted form. Or it could simply be a quick and perfunctory method of bringing an encounter to a conclusion.

That is to say that all these rituals can be performed because they are, as we say, the 'done thing'. In other words, they are performed without any real meaning or sincerity behind them.

The same is true of ritual words and actions in religion. That is why the prophets were so critical of those who observed the fasts and feasts and ceremonies of their faith, and yet whose lives, in reality, were quite unaffected by it.

'I hate, I despise your feasts', said Amos, speaking for God. 'I take no delight in your solemn assemblies . . . Take away from me the noise of your hymns; to the melody of your harps I will not listen. But let justice roll down like waters, and righteousness like an ever-flowing stream.'

In the same way Jesus, too, was critical of the Pharisees who placed such emphasis on the ritual of outward cleansing, but were not clean on the inside. And he complained of those who uttered ritual words to him, 'Lord, Lord', but who did not do the things that he said.

It is possible to come to this sacrament and see it simply in terms of the cup. Purely as a ritual, that is, in which we remember Christ's death. And like all ritual actions, it can mean a great deal, or very little.

2 But let's return just for a moment to the business of perception, and to the second picture which we looked at this morning. For we saw that when we looked at it long and hard enough, then our perception shifted, so that what we were seeing, in fact, was not a cup at all, but two faces. And I would suggest that that is what should happen with this sacrament.

I mean, what is this service, and its particular action, all about? Is it really just a piece of ritual? Or is it not about an encounter between two faces? To be even more precise, is it not about Jesus and you – Jesus and ourselves?

The sacrament was not given to us so that we might remember a dead Christ, though it does remind us of how he died, and why he died. 'This is my body which is for you.' 'This cup is the new covenant in my blood which was shed for many.' The sacrament reminds us of the suffering involved in his death, and of the fact that his death was for us.

But we do not celebrate, as Christian people, a Christ whose life ended on a cross. We celebrate a Christ who was raised from the dead, and who lives in triumph. And whose forgiveness and mercy and help and strength and grace and love are still available to us through his Spirit, and available to us even now.

That is why the sacrament is more than a cup. To see it as a piece of ritual involving the use of bread and wine is to miss its full meaning. It is about the bringing together of Jesus, with all his benefits, and ourselves.

'Jesus and you' is the note of this service – Jesus and ourselves! 'Behold, I stand at the door and knock', says the Risen Christ. 'If any man hear my voice and opens the door, I will come in to him, and sup with him, and he with me!' And that is the language of encounter, which is the language of real communion.

The bread and the wine are his way of knocking this morning. The bread and the wine are the stimulus, by which we may respond to his real presence with us, in which he offers his love and forgiveness and grace and strength.

The trouble is that most of us, even here, experience shifting perceptions. Cup or Communion? Ritual or encounter? What do we mean by this service? We can never quite make up our minds.

Nor will we ever, until we set what we do here in a distinctive background. That was the problem, you remember, with the draw-ings we saw this morning. Our perception kept shifting, because the background was unclear. If it was white we saw one thing, but if it was black, we saw another.

The same will always be true of this sacrament. Our perceptions here too will keep shifting, until we set it against the clear back-ground, not of unfaith, but of faith. That is what St Augustine meant when he said 'Crede et manducasti' – 'Believe and thou hast eaten!' He meant that, at the sacrament, the grace of God is mediated through faith to faith.

So if, in the words of the invitation, we do draw near with faith, then the sacrament will become not a ritual but an encounter. For the ritual act will fade, to become a real means of grace by which we come face to face with Christ. And so we will take the bread, he saying to us 'Follow me'. And we responding 'Lord, I will try'. We saying to him 'But Lord, I am sinful'. And he replying 'I will forgive you'. We saying to him 'But Lord, I am weak'. And he responding, 'My strength is yours. And not just here as you come to this table, but through all the changes and chances of life. So go with my peace in your hearts!'

PRAYER

Lord Jesus Christ, when you lived on earth
You met all kinds of people: ˉ
The sick, the sad, the self-righteous, the self-sufficient,
Those who were torn by sin, those who had little sense of sin,
Those who were selfish, those whose generosity knew no
    bounds,
Those who were powerful and respected, those with no self-
    respect,
And you presented a challenge to them all.

Gathered around your table,
Grant that our Communion today
May be not a ritual act
But a real encounter,
And come to meet us in our need
Whatever that may be.

To those who are sad
Grant your comfort,
To those who are anxious
Your peace,
To those who are tempted and weak
Your strength,
To those who cannot forgive themselves for what they have
    been
Your forgiveness,
To those who struggle for goodness
Your endurance.

6

Give those who are self-sufficient
An awareness of their need,
Those who are selfish
A large generosity,
Those who are self-righteous
A knowledge of what real goodness is,
Those who are powerful
A wisdom in its exercise.

Lord, as we commune with you,
Lead all of us to new heights of holy living
And give us the spiritual stamina to attain them.

For your love's sake. Amen

ENOUGH AND TO SPARE

But when he came to himself, he said, 'How many of my father's hired servants have bread enough and to spare, but I perish here with hunger!' LUKE 15.17 (RSV)

It wasn't much fun being a prodigal. At least it wasn't much fun when your resources were gone, and you found yourself friendless among the pigs. For the Jew, that was the lowest rung on the ladder. It was 'the ultimate mark of degradation'.

Yet, unlike many in a similar state, the prodigal was wise enough to see it, and as he reflected on his situation, memories of more felicitous days flooded into his mind. Whatever the restrictions of his father's house, at least there, there had been no shortage. Back at home, not even the casual hands had known the meaning of want. The father's house had had an abundance of supply even for those who performed the most menial of tasks. 'How many of my father's hired servants have bread enough and to spare?'

'Enough and to spare.' This is a very suggestive phrase as we come to the Communion table in the Father's house now. The bread and wine of the sacrament, with all their deep and rich symbolism, demonstrate the ample provision of the Father. There is nothing stinting in his giving, no poverty in his providing. This table speaks of the Father's abundance, of the Father who gives 'enough and to spare'.

1 'Enough and to spare' of the father's *forgiving love*. This is what the prodigal discovered first of all as he rounded the corner and caught his first distant glimpse of the old homestead. Any fears which he might have nourished about his reception were dispelled immediately. 'For while he was yet afar off, his father saw him, and ran and fell on his neck and kissed him.' And these visible tokens of the father's love, these tangible signs of the father's forgiveness, were all the assurance the prodigal needed.

In his novel *Cry, the Beloved Country*, Alan Paton tells of a black

8

African priest, Stephen Kumalo, who sets out for Johannesburg in search of his son from whom he has not heard for years. Arriving, he discovers that the boy has fallen into evil ways, and the deeper he suspects the trouble to be, the more intensely he searches for him, until he eventually finds him in prison charged with the murder of a white man. The old man takes his son's hand in both his own, and the hot tears fall fast upon them . . . 'My child, my child . . . At last I have found you'. For Kumalo's son, the tears of the old priest; for the prodigal, the open arms and embrace: how eloquently they spoke to each of his father's forgiving love. Visible, tangible signs, so that words were superfluous.

No one is ever worthy to come to this table, but we cannot doubt our reception as we do come, for the symbols of the feast are the visible, tangible tokens of the Father's forgiving love – 'enough and to spare'. These symbols are a reminder of our Lord's passion. That is to say, they remind us of the event of the cross, which was the supreme manifestation of the Father's forgiving love.

Of course, for centuries men had realized that God was forgiving. Was it not the psalmist who had said 'If thou, O Lord, shouldest mark iniquities, Lord, who could stand? But there is forgiveness with thee'? And was it not Jeremiah who spoke of a time coming, when God would say to his people, 'I will forgive your iniquity, and your sin I will remember no more'? These were wonderful insights into the character of God. But never in their wildest dreams could men have conceived a love such as was revealed in the incarnate suffering Son on Golgotha – a love which knew no bounds, no restrictions, no limits, a love which not even man's cruelty and folly and wickedness could destroy.

All this we remember at the Communion table. The bread and wine are the visible, tangible tokens of the Father's forgiving love – 'enough and to spare' – and as we take them we may, in the words of Horatius Bonar,

> . . . lay aside each earthly load
> And taste afresh the calm of sins forgiven.

2 'Enough and to spare' of the Father's *restoring grace*. This is the second thing the prodigal discovered when he returned.

How well he had prepared himself for that moment of meeting, and doubtless all the way home was rehearsing that speech about his unworthiness to be a son, and his plea to be accepted as a hired servant.

But the plea was never made, for the father interrupted him. This pitiful creature standing before him, beneath the wrinkles of high living and the marks of sin, is still recognizable to the father as his boy. He is a son, however dim the bedraggled resemblance may be, and the symbols of sonship will be restored to him. The best robe to cover his rags; a ring – the sign that he is still an heir; shoes – the token of sonship, as opposed to the barefooted slaves. All are lavishly bestowed with urgency. 'For this my son was dead, and is alive again: he was lost, and is found.'

Whatever else this sacrament means, it means that God not only accepts us with his pardon, but also with his restoring grace. However weak, however foolish, however unworthy, he welcomes us to the table in his house, still seeing in us resemblance to himself – high hopes, perhaps, aspirations for cleanness and wholeness, so that the Father's features, although eroded, are not altogether eradicated. And with the robe of his righteousness, he covers the rags of our unrighteousness, accepts us at the table of his Son, and receives us, not as slaves but as children and heirs.

This was the great thought of the apostle Paul: 'You did not receive the spirit of slavery . . . but you have received the spirit of sonship . . . and if children, then heirs, heirs of God and fellow heirs of Christ.'

Franz Kafka's *Metamorphosis*, a parable on the reaction to suffering, tells of a young salesman who awakens one morning hideously changed into the form of a giant insect, although still retaining human feelings and intellect. The story is concerned with the response of the family – father, mother and sister – to his transformation. Initially, while shocked and pitiful, they are happy that he remains apart from them, a prisoner in his room. But the pity eventually changes into loathing, revulsion and abandonment, and the gradual desire for Gregor's demise.

How utterly foreign that is to the picture of God. However marred the resemblance to the Father in us, the wonder is that he receives us with his restoring grace – 'enough and to spare', by receiving us at this table as his children.

3 'Enough and to spare' of the father's *continual sustenance*. This also the prodigal discovered on his return. His hope had been to return as a hired servant. That is, in the capacity of a casual labourer, a servant who was simply hired on a day-to-day basis. And while such a prospect

was better than feeding on carob pods, it was nevertheless a hand-to-mouth existence, with no guarantee of regular provision.

But accepted as a son, the whole outlook changes and, like the elder brother, he will enjoy the father's abundance.

This table, too, speaks of the Father's provision of continual sustenance. We take the bread and hear the words 'This is my body which is for you', and remember also those other words of Jesus, 'I am the bread of life. He who comes to me shall *never* hunger.' And down the ages men and women have found it so, wherever this sacrament has been celebrated, from private chapel to prison cell.

Listen to Pastor Niemoeller, preaching a Communion sermon to a handful of fellow-Christian prisoners in a cell in Dachau:

> We who are here coming to this table: a small company, each of us forcibly separated from home and loved ones, all of us deprived of our freedom, all of us in uncertainty, not knowing what the coming day – or hour – will bring forth! We eat and drink at our Father's table, and we may be of good courage.

It is the testimony of many centuries long that men and women have found at this table 'trust for their trembling and hope for their fears'; have found that food which sustains the soul through all the vicissitudes of life; for here above all, we are nourished with the very life of God himself – 'enough and to spare'.

Such plenitude we are offered now, as we come to the table – 'Enough and to spare' of the Father's forgiving love. 'Enough and to spare' of the Father's restoring grace. 'Enough and to spare' of the Father's continual sustenance – 'Therefore draw near with faith, and take this holy sacrament to your comfort.'

PRAYER

Father,
We praise and give you thanks,
For your goodness never fails
And your bounty never ceases.

Your word from of old
Has been 'Listen you thirsty ones,
Come to the waters.

11

And you that have no money,
Come, buy and eat.
Yea, come, buy wine and milk
Without money and without price.'

Father, even in our sinfulness,
You meet us with abundance,
So that however far we have wandered,
Whatever the depths of sin into which we have sunk,
No matter how marred the divine image in us,
You welcome us with arms wide open
When we return to you.

Father, even in our unworthiness
You meet us in abundance
For, once returned,
You do not hold us afar off,
But, accepted in the beloved,
Treat us as sons, with all the privileges of sonship
A place in the family of faith
And the right to be present at this table
With its costly provision.

Father, even in our weakness
You meet us in abundance,
For all the riches of your grace
Are ours now and through all the changing circumstances of
    life.
Forgiveness for the past,
Strength for the present
Hope for the future,
And, in the end,
Your nearer presence.

Father for your lovingkindness
May we and all your children
Praise you now and always,
Not only with our lips
But with lives which are well pleasing to you.

Through Jesus Christ our Lord. Amen

PROMISING GOD, UNPROMISING MAN

*After the same manner also he took the cup . . . saying, 'This cup is
the new covenant in my blood.'* 1 CORINTHIANS 11.25

Is it ever right to break a promise? The question was asked of a class in
Moral Philosophy, when I was a student in Glasgow many years ago.
Looking around at my colleagues, I saw many heads shaking, as was
my own. The clear verdict of the majority was that a promise once
made is inviolable. Then the professor posited a hypothetical situation. Just suppose you had promised a man the loan of a shotgun in
two days' time. But on the next day you discovered that the man had
become deranged. Would it be right in these circumstances to break a
promise? Nobody was sure any longer!

Mercifully, that is the kind of situation which few of us are likely to
meet, and we do feel that, in normal circumstances, promises are
made to be honoured. Few would agree with Jonathan Swift when he
said 'Promises and pie crusts are made to be broken'. That kind of
attitude does not beget trust. A promise is, quite literally, something
which is *foresent*. The spoken or written word is a guarantee of action
to follow. Without an understanding of that nature, meaningful life
would be impossible.

1 Ours is a promising God. The God revealed in the Scriptures is
a God who makes promises and keeps them. In fact the very word
testament – Old and New Testament – means 'covenant' or promise.
The whole book bears witness to a promising God.

Sometimes, in the Bible, the promise of God is made to an individual. So God made a covenant, for example, with the patriarchs,
Abraham, Isaac and Jacob. Indeed the same covenant was made,
separately, with all three. It was a promise that God would bless him
and his descendants, that he would be their God and that he would
give them a land where they would live as his people.

But the one great promise of the Old Testament, which gives the

13

collected volume its name, was not made to an individual. It was made to a whole nation of Abraham's descendants. These people had been enslaved in Egypt, had managed to make a miraculous escape, and had come, in their flight, to a place called Sinai. Their incredible deliverance from Pharaoh, they knew to have been the work of God. It was God's hand which had set them free. He was their Liberator. And there, at Sinai, they made a solemn covenant with him, and he with them.

That covenant was really a promise which was mutually binding, so long as both parties were faithful to it. For their part, the people recognized Jahweh as their only God, and agreed to obey his laws. The promise of God was that he would bless them, guide and care for them.

And how faithful to his promise God proved to be! He promised to lead them. And he did not fail. He promised that they would reach their new land. And he did not fail. He promised that they would take possession of it. And he did not fail. God showed himself to be utterly trustworthy.

But Israel's was a sorry story, for while God kept his promise, the people failed to honour theirs. All the way to the Promised Land they complained and grumbled. Indeed, once they had possessed it and settled in it, the story of the nation was one long story of unfaithfulness. They ignored God's laws. They even worshipped other gods. That is why the prophets, in succession, accused them century after century. They were an unfaithful bride. They were a wife who had played the harlot with many lovers. To the faithful Jahweh, they had been unfaithful times without number.

Do you remember, as a child, the dreaded day when you had to go home with a school report in your hand and present it to your parents? How our chest swelled with pride, when the words were written, 'Shows promise'. That was the sign of glowing prospects, and our parents shared our pride. But how ashamed we were, when the words were scrawled, 'Shows little promise'. That was a condemnation. It meant that our efforts to date did not bode well for the future. Our prospects were poor.

That was the problem God found in his people. He had made his promise and kept it. In both the sense of keeping his promises and of offering his people the brightest of prospects, he was a promising God. But the people, on the other hand, had shown little promise.

Indeed, to the promising God, unfaithful Israel had proved singularly unpromising.

I think we all know something of Israel's problem. We have discovered it for ourselves. I mean, how easy it is, especially in times of crisis, to make promises to God. And then the situation passes, and in the return to normal living the vows are forgotten. We discover, like Israel, how unpromising we are at fulfilling the promises of the solemn hour.

That was the difficulty with a covenant based on law. The law said 'Do this and this. Behave in this way. Then you will stand in a right relationship with God, and you will enjoy his favour.' But the people found that their ability did not measure up to the law's demands. And how then could they ever enjoy a right relationship with God?

That is why Jeremiah, one of the greatest of the prophets, looked to a day when God would establish a new covenant with his people, and a different kind of covenant altogether. Speaking for God, he says:

> Behold the days are coming, when I will make a new covenant with the house of Israel, not like the covenant which I made with their fathers when I took them by the hand and led them out of Egypt . . . But this is the covenant which I will make . . . I will put my law within them, and I will write it upon their hearts; and I will be their God and they will be my people . . . For they shall all know me, from the least of them to the greatest; for I will forgive their iniquity, and I will remember their sin no more. (Jeremiah 31.31–4)

That is to say that Jeremiah saw a day coming, when the ever-promising God would perform a new redemptive act. Once again he would call his people from captivity, as he had done before. And in that day he would forgive their sins, making a new covenant with them, and inscribe his law, not on tables of stone, but on the hearts of people moved by gratitude for what he had done.

2 So the centuries passed away. Then in the fullness of time, God sent forth his Son. And in a far more wonderful way than Jeremiah could ever have imagined, God made himself known. Aware that unpromising man cannot establish a right relationship with him, God comes himself, in Jesus, to establish it.

It was to unpromising man that Jesus came. It was among

15

unpromising men that he preached and taught and healed. And it was to unpromising men that he spoke in the Upper Room when, cup in hand, he said, 'This is my blood of the covenant, which is poured out for many for the forgiveness of sins'.

That was a tremendous promise. It was a promise that his imminent death had a purpose. It would accomplish something. Its effect would be forgiveness, the pardon of sin. So here was the new covenant for which Jeremiah longed. It did not repudiate the law. But by it, God's love and favour was no longer conditional on sinlessness, which is what the law demanded. The new covenant was based on grace. That is to say, on God's forgiving love declared in the death of Jesus.

Paul grasped the very heart of it when he said in wonder, 'God commendeth his love toward us, in that, while we were yet sinners, Christ died for us'. That is the wonderful thing about the new covenant. It is God's promise of forgiving love to unpromising man. What was it that John Newton sang?

> Amazing grace, how sweet the sound
> That saved a saint like me?

Not a bit of it. Would that really have been so amazing? As Paul said himself, 'For a good man, one might even choose to die'.

> Amazing grace, how sweet the sound
> That saved a *wretch* like me.

That is what John Newton sang. And that was the extraordinarily amazing thing which Paul, too, found so incredible. The cross was the manifestation of God's forgiving love, not to righteous men, not to good men, but to men and women in the wretched condition of their sinfulness. It was his way of restoring unpromising man to a promising relationship with himself. His forgiving love is the assurance of sinners, now and for the future.

John Donne made the point in his *Hymne to God the Father*:

> Wilt Thou forgive that sinne where I begunne,
> Which is my sinne, though it were done before?
> Wilt Thou forgive those sinnes, through which I runne
> And do runne still: though still I do deplore?
> When Thou hast done, Thou hast not done,
>   For I have more.

16

Wilt Thou forgive that sinne by which I have wonne
Others to sinne? and made my sinne their doore?
Wilt Thou forgive that sinne that I did shunne
A yeare or two: but wallowed in a score?
When Thou hast done, Thou hast not done,
    For I have more.

I have a sinne of feare, that when I have spunne
My last thred, I shall perish on the shore;
Sweare by Thy Selfe, that at my death Thy Sonne
Shall shine as He shines now, and heretofore;
And, having done that, Thou hast done;
    I feare no more.

John Donne (1572–1631)

We need not fear. To you and me, unpromising as our lives may have been, that is what he has foresworn. He will forgive sinful men and women. We have his promise on it. 'This cup is the new covenant in my blood.'

But a covenant is still a two-way agreement. That is to say that to take the cup, the sign of the new covenant, is not only to hear his pledge and be reminded of his gracious promises. It is also to make our own.

And what is our pledge? It is to commit ourselves anew to him whose sacrifice made the new covenant possible. From gratitude and indebtedness for what he has done, it is to offer an obedience which is the obedience of love. It is to determine, relying on his strength, that our unpromising past will be left behind us. With his law written in our hearts, it is to bind ourselves to keep his commandments, and to follow him into that more promising life to which he has called us, and of which he has left us an example.

To that end we come to the table now, to remember his saving work on our behalf, to hear his gracious promises, and to renew our own to him.

PRAYER

Praise be to you, O God our Father.
Great is your faithfulness.
With you there is no variableness or shadow of turning.
Your love never ends.
Your goodness never ceases.
You never fail to honour your word,
Or to keep your gracious promises.
You are utterly trustworthy.

Father, we praise you,
That when man grieved and disappointed you
With vain expectation,
You did not relinquish hope
Or withhold your love,
But sent your son to save us from sin
And draw us to you.

Praise be to you, Lord Jesus Christ,
That to rescue us from our hopeless situation,
You endured the cross, despising the shame,
And left this sacrament as a memorial of your sacrifice.

Lord, the poverty of our lives,
Our repeated disobedience,
Our continual failure in goodness,
Our forlorn attempts at holy living,
Our unpromising past,
Must constantly wound you.

Holy Spirit of God
Only as we are empowered by you
Can we be what we ought to be
And do what we ought to do.

So, at the table this morning,
Fill us with your Spirit.
Take possession of us
That we may be inspired
To obey your commandments,

18

To love what is good,
And to long for righteousness

That our unpromising past may be put behind us
And our lives may become a thing of beauty
Bringing joy to our God and Father.

Through Jesus Christ our Lord. Amen.

THE NIGHT OF BETRAYAL

*The Lord Jesus, **the same night in which he was betrayed**,
took bread.*   1 CORINTHIANS 11.23 (AV)

Have you ever wondered why St Paul included these words in this passage? Clearly, his real concern is to advise the Corinthians on their proper approach to the Holy Supper, their behaviour at it, and the full meaning of it? So why add the words: 'The Lord Jesus, *the same night in which he was betrayed*, took bread'? It is a phrase which appears almost like an aside, and you can't help wondering whether the apostle was merely imparting some incidental information, or whether he was making a valuable point, of which he wanted his readers to take careful note.

When you read the whole passage, you are driven to the second conclusion. For the one thing which is perfectly obvious, is that St Paul is actually rebuking the Corinthians, scolding them for behaviour at the Lord's table which was making a mockery of the whole proceedings.

This was meant to be a meal where the fellowship was bound together in Christian love – love for Christ and love for each other. But in Corinth that was sadly lacking. There was greed at the table, and pride and self-indulgence, and a glaring disparity between rich and poor, when one man left hungry while another left in a drunken state.

And so, I think, St Paul adds the words, 'The Lord Jesus, the same night in which he was betrayed, took bread', to add force to the rebuke, and thereby to shame the Corinthians into an awareness of their unworthy behaviour. 'Remember,' he seems to say, 'the circumstances in which this meal was first celebrated. It was the night in which he was *betrayed* that it all started.' And how could they ever again perpetuate these abuses, when they recalled the solemn events of that night?

'The Lord Jesus, the same night in which he was betrayed.' A better translation is 'The Lord Jesus, the same night in which he was *being betrayed*'. That gives the sense of something going on simultaneously with his own actions – something going on behind his back, something furtive, something sinister – while he is engaged in these holy things.

At any rate, St Paul felt that the Corinthians would benefit from the reminder that this was the background to the Supper, and it may be profitable for us, too, as we come to the table today, to remind ourselves of those things that Jesus said and did 'in the night in which he was betrayed'.

1. *It was on the night in which he was betrayed, that he washed the feet of his men.*

That happened early in the night when they were at the table, for somehow the customary washing of feet had been omitted. So the situation arose where everyone was saying to himself, 'Who is going to do it? Have *I* got to offer?' And none was willing to put himself out as the servant to the others. Then, John tells us, 'Jesus took a basin and a towel, and began to wash the feet of his disciples'.

It brought an immediate protest from Peter: 'Lord, you will never wash my feet.' And are we not all like Peter in this? Yes, we'll do our bit for the church, and try our best to be good friends and neighbours, and if it is possible to work to earn God's favour, then we will do everything we can. But to admit that we need cleansing by Christ – that is beneath our dignity, far too injuring to our pride and our self-esteem! And yet Jesus insists, in words that Peter and we can only accept, 'Unless I wash you, you have no part in me'.

But there is more, for, turning from Peter he says to them all: 'I have given you an example, that you should also do as I have done to you'. And if we sympathize with Peter's protest, we utterly balk at this idea. 'Lord', we argue, 'you don't know the kind of world we live in. This is a hard, competitive world, where each has to make his own way, and look after number one first. It's a world where you have to trample on others for the sake of getting somewhere, far less wash, each other's feet.'

And yet his command states: 'Do as I have done to you.' And it demands service without pride or discrimination, with one disciple caring for another, even his competitors, his rivals and those who would injure him.

21

And again we protest that this is too much. 'I mean, Lord, look at the kind of people we have to deal with, and we've got to think of our position!' Yet he washed the feet of Peter who denied him, and James and John, the squabbling Sons of Thunder whose chief concern was the first places in the kingdom, and even of Judas whose same feet within minutes were away on the treacherous business of betrayal.

The need for cleansing, and the need to serve as he himself served – these things he taught on the night in which he was betrayed, when he washed the feet of his men.

2 It was on the night in which he was betrayed, that he promised to secure, by his death, a right relationship with God for all men.

'This is my body, which is for you', he said, as he took the bread and broke it. 'This cup is the new covenant in my blood.' And that new covenant meant that, by his death, men could enjoy a relationship with God, not based on law as was the old covenant, but based on God's forgiving love as exemplified in the cross.

During the reign of Elizabeth I, when measures were taken against the Roman Catholic priests trained in the doctrines of the Counter-Reformation, the Jesuit Edmund Campion was arrested while going to celebrate the Mass and, tried by the courts, he was imprisoned and condemned. One night before his death, his cell door opened and a hooded figure entered, begging for forgiveness. The man uncovered his face and Campion saw his betrayer – one of his own familiar friends. And Edmund Campion not only forgave him, but knowing that he too was sought by the authorities, gave him a letter which would ensure him a safe passage to the Continent.

It was on the night

> when doomed to know
> The eager rage of every foe

– when Judas was plotting with the authorities for a price, when the others could not watch with him 'one little hour' in Gethsemane, when Peter dismissed all knowledge of him with curses, when the rest forsook him and fled into the darkness – that was the night on which Jesus broke the bread and poured out the blood-red wine, and vowed that he would provide them and all mankind with the way of safety and salvation – the assurance of God's forgiving love, as seen in his cross.

22

3 *It was on the night in which he was betrayed, that he gave thanks and sang.*

We have it in the words of institution, 'The Lord Jesus . . . took bread, and when he had given *thanks*, he brake it'. And Matthew tells us that when supper had ended, 'they *sang* a hymn, and went out to the Mount of Olives'. How little we understand this Jesus – thanksgiving and praise on the night of his betrayal! Ahead of him was Gethsemane, and his agony and his trial and the scourging and suffering on the cross. And he gives thanks and he sings!

Indeed, if the Last Supper was the Passover meal, then we even know the words he sang – these from Psalm 118:

O give thanks to the Lord, for he is good; for his steadfast love endures forever.

It is almost incredible that in the darkest hour, Jesus was able to praise God for his goodness. Most of us in times of stress find strength in our community. But his own people turned against him. Or we can find support from our family or understanding friends. But his family misunderstood him and his friends deserted him. Everything to provide that staying power, which we all look for in difficult times, was utterly swept away. But the one thing that remained and still gave him cause to praise was his utter faith in God, and his trust that God, would vindicate him.

It is told that when things looked bleak, Martin Luther would say to Melanchthon, 'Come, Philip, let us sing the forty-sixth Psalm, and let them do their worst!' And together they would sing, 'God is our refuge and our strength, a very present help in trouble'. It was the same faith that held Jesus on the night of his betrayal, and which enabled him to thank and to praise.

Understandably, Christian devotion has applied to Jesus the picture of Isaiah's suffering servant – the 'man of sorrows and acquainted with grief'. But in Jesus there was that joy which was deeper than sorrow, and which sprang from his confidence in God.

It was 'on the night in which he was betrayed', says St Paul to the unworthy Corinthians, that the Lord 'took bread'. And unworthy as we are, let us come now to the feast. For here he still offers cleansing, and sends us out in the service of others. Here the bread and wine still remind us of the new covenant, no longer based on law, but on God's

23

infinite grace, as seen in the cross. And we can leave with thanks and praise on our lips for this brave, triumphant faith, in which we can face life and even death, confident that nothing can separate us from the love of God in Jesus Christ, whose presence is granted to us at this table.

PRAYER

Lord Jesus Christ,
We come now to your table
And then we must return to the world
In which you have called us to bear witness to you
And to serve others in your name.

Help us there to follow the example you set us
In that night on which you were betrayed.

Help us to learn from your humility,
So that no sense of our dignity may hinder us,
No false estimate of our value may deter us,
And no foolish pride may hold us back
From the humblest service for you and our fellow men.

Help us to learn from your forgiving love
So that no grudges may be borne,
No bitterness may be harboured,
And no resentment may be nourished
Towards those who, by word and action,
Try to do us harm.

And help us to learn from your irrepressible joy
So that even in our sorest trials,
Even in times of danger and stress,
Even in the face of sorrow and suffering,
We still may praise our God and Father
Because we know that in life or in death we are in his hand.

Lord, help us so to dedicate ourselves to you
In mind and in body
That we may be used for your glory.

For your love's sake. Amen

THE SACRAMENTAL LIFE

I wonder if you watch the 'Songs of Praise' programme on Sunday evenings? If you do, then you may recall a most memorable programme in that series, which was screened some time ago, and designed to mark the centenary celebrations of the Salvation Army.

As one has come to expect of the Army, the music and the singing on the occasion was superb, and enjoyment for the viewer was heightened by the enthusiasm with which the hymns were sung. Few sing their praise with such an expression of joy! But among the hymns chosen on that occasion, there was one which came as something of a surprise to me, because the background to its theme was the Lord's Supper. Set to the haunting tune 'Spohr', the words written by Albert Orsborn are these:

> My life must be Christ's broken bread,
> My love his outpoured wine.
> A cup o'erfilled, a table spread
> Beneath his name and sign.
> That other souls, refreshed and fed,
> May share his life through mine.

The words could make the hymn very suitable for inclusion in a Communion service. That, in fact, is why the choice was so surprising, because one thing which the Salvation Army does not do, on principle, is celebrate the Christian sacraments.

Yet, however suitable the words might seem, the hymn really reflects a belief about the sacraments which is shared, not just by the Salvation Army, but also by the Quakers, the Society of Friends. It is the conviction that the whole of life is sacramental, so that the natural expression of the faith is not in the performance of ritual actions at all, but in the service of God's children in the world. Having said that, however, one would hasten to add that while neither group participates in the external celebration of the sacrament, both testify, nevertheless, to the reality of the experience which we call 'communion'.

25

Those of us who worship within the mainstream churches do celebrate the sacrament. Indeed, it is central to our worship. And sometimes it is useful to remind ourselves of why this should be so.

1 In the first place, the sacrament is central to our worship, because Jesus commanded it. It was Jesus himself who specifically requested that his followers would repeat his action.

'Do this', he said to his disciples in the Upper Room, 'in remembrance of me.' And the present imperative of the verb, '*do this*', in the Greek, suggests that the more accurate translation is '*keep on doing this*'. Indeed, the notion of perpetuity is reinforced by St Paul in his letter to the church at Corinth where, in words which have become known as the 'words of the institution' of the sacrament, he informs the Corinthians that the sacrament is to be continued 'until he come'.

The Scottish paraphrase captures the intention perfectly:

Through latest ages, let it pour
In memory of my dying hour.

The command of our Lord was that the action of the sacrament was not just to be shared there and then in the Upper Room, but was to be perpetuated by succeeding generations of disciples. That is how the injunction was understood by the New Testament Church, as the Acts of the Apostles and the epistles amply demonstrate, while the *Didache*, which describes the worship of the Early Church in the post-New-Testament period, and the writings of the Early Fathers, reveal no deviation from that understanding.

Now it was never the way of Jesus to encumber men and women with ritual which was not beneficial. The observance of ritual acts which did not elevate the heart and mind and character to God, he utterly abhorred. He despised the ritual washings and cleansings of the Pharisees, for example, as long as they did not produce a corresponding cleanliness of heart. And he referred to the scribes and Pharisees who paid their ritual tithes, but neglected the more important matters of the law – justice, mercy and fidelity – as 'blind guides, who strain out a gnat and swallow a camel!'

How well Jesus knew that a man can perform all the ritual actions which his religion demands, and yet still be as remote in heart from God as the sun is from the earth! The Pharisee who prayed outside the temple was like that. He kept a fast twice a week. He offered to

26

God a tenth of whatever came his way. All the ritual acts he performed impeccably. But it was the despised Publican and not the self-righteous Pharisee who left the temple justified before God.

Jesus deprecated ritual for its own sake. He had no time whatsoever for useless and unprofitable ceremonies. Yet it was the same Jesus who, with his men gathered around a table, took bread and wine, and said 'Do this', laying the perpetual obligation of this sacrament on his disciples. The conclusion must be, therefore, that he had good reason for doing it, and that obedience to his dying command would be to their benefit and ours.

So when we come to the Holy Table to set forth this memorial, we do it to comply with the will of Jesus. We do it because he commanded us to do it, knowing that compliance with his instruction would be for our spiritual welfare. We do it in obedience to him.

2 Another reason for the centrality of this sacrament is that by its very simple action, the sharing of broken bread and poured out wine, it takes us to the very heart of our faith. For the sacrament is a vivid reminder of our Lord's death.

It was not just his birth, his teaching, his life, that Jesus wanted to have remembered. He wanted his death to be remembered particularly, and the sacrament was the means which he appointed to do it.

But why should anyone choose to have his death remembered? The reason was that his death had tremendous significance for us all, and St Paul expressed that significance very simply when he wrote not just that 'Christ gave himself', but that he 'gave himself for our sins'.

That is what the symbolism of this sacrament represents so vividly. As we take it we remember *how* he 'gave himself'. The broken bread and the blood-red wine speak eloquently of that:

> the cruel nails, the crown of thorns
> And Jesus crucified . . .

But the words of the sacrament remind us of something even more intimate and personal:

> the cruel nails, the crown of thorns
> And Jesus crucified *for me.*

'This is my body which is for *you.*' 'This cup is the new covenant in my blood which is poured out for many.' The sacrament is a vivid reminder and representation, not only of *how* he gave himself, but of

27

why he gave himself. He gave himself for our sins. He died to do something for us which we could not do for ourselves. He died so that we might enter that new world of eternal life, and so put an end to the world of self and sin which he allowed to put an end to him.

In his novel *The Citadel*, A. J. Cronin told the story of Andrew Manson, a brilliant young doctor who, full of ideals about caring and service, takes up practice as a general practitioner in the Welsh valleys. After struggling to make ends meet, however, he becomes dissatisfied, and eventually moves to a practice in London. There he meets doctors whose standards are quite different from his own, and who, from their private clinics, fare sumptuously by playing on the hypochondria of the wealthy. He begins to follow their ways and to share in their prosperity, and while he does it, at first, with an uneasy conscience, soon their practices, attitudes and assumptions become quite acceptable to him.

But one day, says Cronin, 'the bolt fell'. For, having referred to one of these doctors a shopkeeper whom he has known for years, Manson watches aghast as the 'specialist' bungles an operation during which the patient dies. Then, as he is confronted by the grief and the innocent suffering of the shopkeeper's widow, he comes to his senses. And eventually, although it involves a change in his whole lifestyle, the 'citadel' is rebuilt and his ideals are restored.

Is that not, at least in part, why Jesus wanted his death remembered? The cross exposes the folly of our sin. The suffering endured there, by the innocent, selfless and wholly sinless one, reveals the consequence of our selfish and sinful living. It says, in effect, 'That is what sin does'. The cross is the 'bolt falling', to bring us to our senses, and to hold out to us the possibility of a life of a different quality. Was that not, in fact, precisely what Paul was saying, when he wrote to the members of the church in Galatia: 'Christ gave himself for our sins to deliver us from the present evil age, according to the will of our God and Father'?

The sacrament is central to us because it reminds us that right at the heart of our faith, is a cross. For the action of the Supper provides a vivid representation of the action of God, in Jesus, not only giving himself, but giving himself for our sins, to deliver us.

3 Again, we celebrate the sacrament, and it is central to our worship, because Communion, far from proving a substitute for service, is, in fact, a stimulus to service.

It is impossible to come to this table without remembering that it was on the night of the Last Supper that Jesus took a basin and towel and girded himself, and washed the feet of his disciples, telling them that he was setting them an example which they had to follow. It is impossible to contemplate the self-giving of Christ on our behalf, of which this sacrament so compellingly reminds us, without finding the inspiration and motivation for our self-giving for others. It is impossible to experience 'communion' with the Christ, who was so moved with compassion for human need and suffering, without having our sympathy similarly enlarged.

In *The Imitation of Christ*, Thomas à Kempis, speaking of the benefits of the sacrament, had a great thought: 'For who, approaching to the fountain of sweetness, does not carry away thence some little sweetness? Or who standing near a great fire, does not receive from it some little heat?'

To come to this table is to expose our lives to the gracious influence of Christ; and as we do that, the springs of compassion are replenished within us. Celebration and service go together. The one is the inspiration of the other. And so it has always been.

Just at the time when the Roman empire was disintegrating, St Jerome, along with others, was running a monastery in Bethlehem. They were days of violence and terror and, for the sake of escaping the barbarian hordes, refugees came flooding into the Holy Land by their thousands.

Jerome, later, was writing of the time, and he said: 'I had to give up writing my commentary on Ezekiel, and nearly all my study. The crowds of homeless made me want to turn the words of scripture into deeds, not just saying holy things, but doing them.'

At this Communion table, we meet the Christ who 'came not to be served but to serve, and to give his life as a ransom for many', and we remember that to follow him means 'not only saying holy things, but doing them'. Thus our Communion, if it is a real Communion, will take us to that point of commitment where we too will not be content to sing, but moved to translate into concrete deeds, the words of the hymn with which I began:

> My life must be Christ's broken bread,
> My love his outpoured wine.
> A cup o'erfilled, a table spread
> Beneath his name and sign.
> That other souls, refreshed and fed,
> May share his life through mine.

29

PRAYER

Lord Jesus Christ,
We come to this table
Because you commanded us to do it
In remembrance of you.

Not to share in a meaningless ritual,
Nor to repeat empty words and actions,
Not to indulge in shallow sentiment
Do we do it,
But because you gave us this memorial
For our good.

Lord, we cannot take the bread and wine
Without remembering
That you came to seek and to save the lost,
That you gave your life a ransom for many,
That you loved us and gave yourself for us.

We cannot take the bread and wine
Without realizing
How appalling all our sinfulness is,
How it grieved the heart of God,
How it cost your very life,
Your body broken and your blood shed.

We cannot take the bread and wine
Without seeing
That your self-giving is a rebuke to our self-seeking,
That your compassion is a reproof to our self-interest,
That your love so freely given challenges our self-concern.

Risen Lord,
By your spirit
You are with us still
To challenge, to inspire,
To strengthen, to support and to guide.

So by our Communion today
Swell within us the springs of pity and compassion,
To feel with others in their need.

Inspire us to follow your example
Of humble and patient service,
So that you may work
In us and through us.

For your love's sake. Amen

ALL ENCOMPASSING LOVE

. . . power to comprehend with all the saints what is the breadth and length and height and depth, and to know the love of Christ which surpasses knowledge. EPHESIANS 3.18–19 (RSV)

In a tribute to her husband Robert, Elizabeth Barrett Browning, whose marriage rescued her from a stern and dominating father, and a restricted life in a darkened sickroom, wrote,

> How do I love thee? Let me count the ways.
> I love thee to the depth and breadth and height
> My soul can reach . . .
> I love thee freely, as men strive for Right.
> I love thee purely, as they turn from Praise.
> . . . I love thee with the breath,
> Smiles, tears, of all my life! – and, if God choose,
> I shall but love thee better after death.

Thinking on one who brought mankind a greater deliverance, Paul prayed that the Ephesians might grasp the vastness of the love of Jesus. Then, as if standing on some vantage point from which he could scan the world, he describes the dimensions of that love. 'It's as high as the farthest star in the sky', he says. 'It's as deep as the deepest depths of the ocean.' 'It's as wide as the widest horizon. The love of Christ is as infinite as that.'

Nowhere is that love focused more sharply in one single action, than at the Communion table. For the bread and wine are a constant reminder of the breadth and depth and length of his love.

1 *The sacrament speaks of the **breadth** of his love*

How particular all our human love is, and to how small a circle it is usually confined! Most of us tend to associate with people of like tastes and interests and ideas, and how easily we dismiss those whose background and outlook and opinions differ from our own.

The disciples of Jesus were no different. Their outlook was narrow and parochial. They were hidebound by prejudice and social convention. But Jesus opened their eyes to new horizons, for his love was all-inclusive, and there was nothing constricting about it. The unclean leper, whom no one would touch, the tax-gatherer, whose company no one wanted, the Samaritan woman, with whom the Jews had no dealings, all found fellowship with him. The love of Jesus transcended every boundary, every tabu, every social convention, and none were excluded from his friendship.

But the scope of Jesus' love was wider still. I wonder if you have ever travelled in an aeroplane and, on the descent for landing, found yourself enveloped in cloud. Then, suddenly, the cloud breaks, and below you is a city teeming with life – cars, buses, shops, factories, and the tiny dots of people in their thousands milling around. Just in that moment, you are suddenly transported from preoccupation with a few people sitting around you, to a whole city pulsing with life, and you want to be out of your limited sphere, and to become a part of it.

That was the kind of expanded vista which Jesus gave his men, for the scope of his love was for the world. That night in the Upper Room, when he broke the bread and passed the cup, he said 'This cup is the new covenant in my blood which is shed for *many*'. And so they were reminded that his love was not just for them or their nation, not just for good people, or even for people who loved him, but for men and women of every condition under heaven.

And whenever you and I, in the narrow worlds we create for ourselves, forget the needy world around us, or allow our prejudices to make us bigoted and intolerant, or restrict our care and concern to our own little circle of family and friends and neighbours, we need to be reminded of his vision of the '*many*'. For the sacrament speaks of the breadth of his love.

2 *The sacrament speaks of the **depth** of his love*

Nobody can come to this table without remembering how the rite began. It was on the night of his betrayal that Jesus gathered his men around him. It was while the forces of evil, within and without, were planning his downfall. It was while the shadow of the cross was breaking into stark reality, that Jesus took bread and wine and spoke of his death. And the question has to be asked – what was the point of it?

I remember reading somewhere of how human sacrifice was ended on Formosa. A young Chinese governor had been appointed and, utterly deploring the practice, he had managed to convince some of the evil of it. But eventually, a severe period of drought came, and the religious leaders pleaded for the appeasement of the gods by the old and tried method of offering a human life. At length the governor conceded, provided that he himself might select the victim, who, he agreed, would be sent to the sanctuary dressed in a full robe and hooded. The morning for the sacrifice came, and the man duly arrived and, as before, the priest raised his knife and the victim fell dead. But when they uncovered the man, they found the young governor. And so, by one man's giving of himself, the horror of the practice was exposed, and human sacrifice on Formosa was ended.

The cross of Jesus demonstrates, on the one hand, the terrible nature of sin. It shows how hideous all our sin is. But even more, because 'God was in Christ reconciling the world to himself', it demonstrates a love which refuses to let men go, in spite of their sin, showing that nothing can separate us from the love of God.

That is why the hymn writer, thinking of the cross, says:

> O love of God! O sin of man!
> In this dread act your strength is tried;
> And victory remains with love:
> Jesus, our Lord, is crucified.

There is no greater extent to which love can go, than to offer itself for the object loved. Jesus said that himself: 'Greater love has no man than this, that a man lay down his life for his friends.' And as he spoke, so he lived and died. But the utterly amazing thing, as St Paul reminds us, is that Christ died for us, not while we were friends, but sinners!

So, at this table, we remember that this is the depth of the love that engulfs us, a love as deep as the cross of Jesus, a love for sinful men and women, as real as the bread and wine. The sacrament speaks of the depth of his love.

John's Gospel says of Jesus at the Last Supper that 'Having loved his own who were in the world, he loved them to the end'. That is precisely what Jesus did. That was the length of his love.

Sometimes as you read the Gospels, that is a cause for wonder. Was he never tempted to break with them, or to seek out others in their place? But no: in spite of their doubts and squabbles and blunders and almost consistent inability to understand him, he had gone on loving them, and would continue to do so.

And now, when he 'earnestly desired' to eat the Passover with them, he gave them the familiar provision, but attaching to the bread and wine a new significance, he related these to the cross which lay ahead, pointing out that this – his final action – was for them.

The pages of history and literature are strewn with the record of man's fickleness, and the story of broken love and infidelity. There is a passage in Shakespeare's *Hamlet*, where Ophelia, realizing that his love for her is gone, attempts to return to Hamlet the love tokens which he has given her in the past. Hamlet replies defensively, 'I never gave thee aught'. And Ophelia replies,

> My honoured lord, you know right well you did;
> And with them, words of so sweet breath composed
> As made the things more rich: their perfume lost,
> Take these again; for to the noble mind
> Rich gifts wax poor, when givers prove unkind.

At the Last Supper, Jesus gave his men tokens of his love. Simple things they were – just bread and wine. And with them he uttered words 'of so sweet breath composed' – 'This is my body which is for you. This cup is the new covenant in my blood, which is shed for many for the remission of sins.' But when Jesus gave these tokens, they were a pledge of his love to the end, and for all time. Indeed, that continuing love was confirmed in his resurrection appearances, and his promise to 'be with them always, even to the end of the age'. The sacrament speaks of the length of his love.

The prayer of St Paul was that the Christian people in Ephesus 'might comprehend the breadth and length and height and depth, and know the love of Christ which surpasses knowledge'. God grant that our Communion today may lead us to that comprehension, and through it, to a response of unflinching loyalty and obedience, in gratitude for his love for us.

PRAYER

Lord, your love for mankind and for us today
Is breathtaking.
We can only gasp and marvel
When we consider that you cared and care for us
As much as your suffering and death reveal.

Lord, as we take the bread and wine,
Fill us with love and devotion to you,
So that we may honour you with purer lives,
With deeper reverence,
And with a greater compassion in the service of others.

Lord, by the width of your love,
Teach us to care, as you cared,
For the unloved and the unlovely,
For the ungrateful and the ungracious,
For the unhelpful and the unkind.

Lord, by the depth of your love,
Teach us to care, as you cared,
Where caring hurts,
Where caring is costly,
Where caring demands sacrifice.

Lord, by the length of your love,
Teach us to care, as you cared,
When we are tempted to give up,
When our patience is sorely tried,
When more is asked of us than we have to give.

Lord, by our communion here,
Strengthen us to follow your example,
Who came not to be served, but to serve,
And to give your very all for our sake.

Lord, hear our prayer. Amen

THE THREE PERSPECTIVES OF THE LORD'S SUPPER

*'This do in remembrance of me. . . .' For as often as you eat this
bread and drink this cup, you proclaim the Lord's death until he
come.* 1 CORINTHIANS 11.24–26

These verses, which almost certainly give the earliest account we
have of the institution of this sacrament, are especially valuable for a
number of reasons. For one thing, the words are probably the earliest
record of any saying of Jesus. They also make it clear that it is the
Church's ongoing duty to continue this sacrament and, whereas the
Gospels do not mention it, they tell us that the Communion service
has to be perpetuated 'until he come'. In fact, were it not for these
words of St Paul set down in a pastoral letter to the church at Corinth,
we might otherwise have been unaware of what I have chosen to call
the 'three perspectives' of the Lord's sacrament.

What are these three perspectives?

1 First of all, these words of institution bid us to look backwards.
'This do', said Jesus, 'in *remembrance* of me.'

The New Testament word for remembrance is *anamnesis* (we see
our word 'amnesia' in it), and it means 'the activity of calling to
mind'. So, at the Lord's Supper we deliberately gather to look back,
to call to mind, to remember Jesus.

But is that activity as simple as it seems, and how in fact *do* we
remember Jesus?

Nowadays we live in a world in which all kinds of sophisticated
gadgets greatly facilitate the process of remembering: cameras, for
instance, which, by an ingenious process, develop the picture on the
spot; transistorized pocket-width micro-recorders; and, of late, the
ubiquitous video camera. All kinds of devices enable us to capture
events which we wish to treasure, and provide the means to recall
them whenever we so desire.

What wife is not to be found now and again thumbing over the

37

pages of the wedding album and remembering, or gazing at the first photograph of the children after they were born, or the picture of their first school day? And what family ever tires of watching the capers of the summer holiday, captured with the aid of a video camera? To the outsider looking on, they might be dull and amateurish efforts, but for us, they help to recall some cherished moments of the past, and we enter into the experience and re-live it again, as we remember.

That is precisely how the symbols of the sacrament help us today. Jesus, too, wanted to be remembered. In particular, he wanted his death to be remembered, and to aid us in recalling these solemn events, he give us these symbols of bread and wine. 'Take, eat', he said, 'this is my body which is for you.' 'This cup is the new covenant in my blood. This do ye, as oft as ye drink it, in remembrance of me.'

So, in obedience to his command, we take the cup and drink the blood-red wine and, as we do, we look back and remember and

> . . . try to see
> The cruel nails, and crown of thorns,
> And Jesus crucified for me.

For the outsider, looking on, the ritual may be quite unimpressive and the symbols may mean little or nothing, but for the person who comes in faith, they become not only a means to aid the memory, but a way to the very presence of Christ and the experience of Communion with his Lord, whose sufferings he recalls at this table.

2 But the words of institution which bid us to look backwards, also summon us to the present. 'This *do*', said Jesus, 'in remembrance of me.'

In the original Greek the force of this is not simply, 'Do this', but 'Keep on doing this'. It is a command to perpetuate the sacrament. So the instruction of Jesus is that, now and for all time, as long as the faithful gather, they are to take bread and wine and 'do this'.

But this passage also makes clear *why* we are to do it, and why we are to keep on doing it. The reason is that by so doing we are making a proclamation – an acted proclamation of the Lord's death. 'For as often as you eat this bread and drink this cup, you proclaim the Lord's death.'

One of the names applied to the Lord's Supper in the early

reformed Scottish Church was the 'action'. So it was described in Knox's Book of Common Order, and almost a century later, in the Westminster Directory for public worship, 'the minister is to begin the *action*, with sanctifying and blessing the elements'. Indeed, until comparatively recent times, the sermon preached immediately before the celebration of the sacrament was known as the 'action sermon'. That name has now fallen into disuse, but at least it had this to be said for it, that it preserved the present sense – the 'this do now' of the sacrament, and also the sense of its being an acted sermon or an acted proclamation of the death of our Lord.

'Do this', said Jesus. 'Keep on doing this', and, as we obey his words and keep this sacrament, we proclaim to sinful men and women the love of God, seen at its highest in the sacrificial death of Jesus.

> For lo! between our sins and their reward
> We set the Passion of thy Son our Lord.

3 But the sacrament which bids us look backwards to remember Christ and his sufferings for us, and which summons us in the present to repeat continually this action, also has a future perspective. 'For as often as you eat this bread and drink this cup, you proclaim the Lord's death, *until he come*.'

'Until he come.' The suggestion is that a time is coming, when there will no longer be a need for this sacrament which calls us to remember him, for he will come and we shall be with him.

That the sacrament should no longer be required, or at least lose its significance in such an event, is a very natural thing. To go back to the photograph again, what soldier in wartime did not carry as one of his most treasured possessions a picture of his wife or mother or family or girlfriend? But when he returned, that frequently-consulted photograph simply became a relic or keepsake, or at least its former significance was lost, because he was now reunited with those whom it had helped him to remember. So the Lord's Supper, while it is vital to us – and it *is* vital as a memorial of the past, and full of strengthening power for the present, no less vital than the soldier's photograph was to him in bringing close to mind his loved ones at home – is nevertheless not of final significance, for it looks forward to a 'fuller communion beyond time itself'.

There is a triumphant eschatological note here, and we miss the full significance of the Lord's Supper unless we sound it, and its strains speak of a day when Christ's people will no longer need a memorial of One who is present with them in person; of a day when the words of Jesus at the very first Communion will be fulfilled: 'I will see you again, and your hearts will rejoice, and no one will take your joy from you'; of a day such as Horatius Bonar saw in his great Communion hymn:

> Feast after feast thus comes and passes by,
> Yet passing, points to the glad feast above;
> Bearing sweet foretaste of the festal joy,
> The Lamb's great bridal feast of bliss and love.

A look at the past, a summons to the present, a glimpse to the future – the sacrament encourages us to do all three. So let us come now to this table – and, here, let us 'remember him', and 'do this', 'until he come'.

PRAYER

Lord, as we worship you.
We thank you for everything that brings you to mind.

For this day with its rest and quiet,
For the Church and its offering of prayers and praise,
For the Bible which records your words and deeds
In the days of your flesh,
And those of your disciples
When they were empowered by the Spirit.

But most of all we thank you
For this sacrament
Whereby our souls are nourished
With the very Bread of Life.

Lord, we thank you
That you chose simple things,
Just bread and wine,
As the sign and seal of your love for us
Given freely on the cross.

40

As we take them this morning,
Make us deeply grateful
For all that you have done,
And for your love which still sustains us.
And may our participation
Be a true proclamation
That you are indeed our Lord and Redeemer,
And a declaration of our intent
To follow you more faithfully in the future.

Lord, we thank you
For the promise of our faith,
For the certainty that one day
We shall enjoy closer communion with you
And with those whom we have loved
Who have died trusting in you.

And to that end,
Urge us on and keep us yours,
Until that day when the veil shall be lifted
And we behold you, face to face.

For your love's sake. Amen

OUR UNITY IN CHRIST

I hear that there are divisions among you. 1 CORINTHIANS
11.18 (RSV)

During the American War of Independence, there was a song which
was sung by those who were prepared to fight for the cause. Written
by John Dickinson, part of it contained the words:

> Then join hand in hand, brave Americans all.
> By uniting we stand, by dividing we fall.

The thing that the apostle Paul found so upsetting about the
members of the church at Corinth, was that as a congregation, they
were divided and in danger of falling. Indeed, when he wrote his first
letter to them, he had to deal with their disunity again and again.

There were members of this church whose whole outlook was
partisan, so that each professed loyalty to a particular teacher. 'I
belong to Paul. I belong to Cephas. I belong to Apollos!' Paul saw how
divisive it was. There was no room for it in the Christian Church. So,
reprimanding them for any claim to a separate allegiance, he reminds
them that, whoever their teachers were, 'all are of Christ'.

There were members of this church who considered themselves
better than others, because they possessed a spectacular gift called
'speaking in tongues'. Indeed, those who practised it regarded those
who did not as spiritually inferior. Paul had no time for such spiritual
snobbery. It created divisions. And he points out that this 'spectacular' gift is no more important than any other, and possibly the least
important of all. Of far greater concern is the unity of the body, and
the contribution which each member, with his or her individual gifts,
is able to make to it.

But when Paul heard of the divisions which occurred at the Lord's
table, he could hardly believe it. How could there possibly be division, here of all places? How could the difference between the

42

wealthy members and the poor, many of whom were slaves, manifest itself at the sacrament? How could barriers of class lead to schism at the sacred meal which Jesus had instituted on the night of his betrayal? Paul was struck to the heart and, hot with righteous indignation, he begins a withering attack on the Corinthians. 'What?' he says, 'Do you despise the church of God and humiliate those who have nothing? Shall I commend you in this? No, I will not!' Then he reminds them of how the Supper began, of what it means, and closes with a warning that 'whoever eats and drinks without discerning the body, eats and drinks judgement on himself'.

Most scholars contend that these words, 'not discerning the body', have a dual meaning. They may refer, on the one hand, to a casual attitude in handling the elements of the sacrament; but equally, and most certainly, they refer to the body of Christ which is the Church. That is to say that we cannot come to the Lord's table without a concern for the sacred thing we are doing, or without a real regard for our fellow Christians within the body of Christ.

'I hear that there are divisions among you.' Paul recognized, of course, that there is a type of division which is quite justifiable and necessary. Without it one could never distinguish the genuine believer from the sham. But when it comes to the Lord's table, he contends that there is never room for division. To forget that, is to incur judgement.

Nothing that we do at the Lord's table can ever be taken lightly. To come to it has the most profound implications.

1 In the first place, to come to this table, is to testify that we are *one in fellowship*.

The Lord's Supper, right from the night of its institution, has always been an act of fellowship. It is the place where Christian people assemble, not as individuals, but as a family. This is what the Corinthians had forgotten. Whatever differences divide us in the world, there is no place from them here. Here, we are one. Class, wealth and position are of no account at all. As George Herbert had it, in *The Temple*:

> Kneeling ne'er spoiled silk stocking; quit thy state;
> All equal are within the Church's gate.

And not only are all equal, but bound together as one. All who come here are friends of our Lord, and therefore friends of one another. At this place above all other, the principle holds good: 'There is neither Jew nor Greek, bond nor free, male nor female. You are all one in Christ Jesus.' You just cannot read what Paul says on the Lord's Supper without noting where he places emphasis and stress. It is on the corporate nature of the rite. It is on the responsibility each has for the care of the other. What we do, we do here as equals, and as one.

Have you ever wondered why, in the Presbyterian tradition, we serve each other with Communion in the pews? It is to preserve these ideas of unity and equality. Our practice, of course, is a development, and, some are surprised to learn, a fairly recent one. In Reformation times, and for the next three hundred years, in Scotland, the custom was for members to give and take the elements sitting around a long table specially erected for Communion. But to serve a whole congregation in relays, even around a large table, could sometimes take the best part of a day. So the current practice was adopted a century ago for the sake of shortening the service. And although that means that the majority now sit in pews, we all sit, nevertheless, around the one table. That is why the practice arose of covering the pews with white cloths. They are symbolic of that one table where we meet as one family, equal and in unity with each other.

The Reformers were adamant about the method. They chose it because to sit around the table was to come as close as possible to the procedure at the Last Supper itself. And the practice of sharing the elements was equally important to them. To give to each other and take from each other was a sign that, at this table, we come as equals in one body.

The Lord's table is the place where we come as one fellowship. To meet here is to be strengthened in love for one another. To meet here is to recognize that we belong to each other through the common bond that unites us. And it is also to realize our essential unity with all who love the name of Christ, with whom we are called into a common fellowship of active service.

2 Secondly, to come to this table is to testify that we are *one in faith*.

That is why we say the Creed together at this service. It is a statement of the faith which we hold in common. It is a declaration of the things which we believe God has done in the past, is doing now, and will do in the future. In fact the whole Supper is a proclamation of our common faith in Jesus Christ as Saviour and Lord. It reminds us of his saving work for us all. And as each of us takes the bread and wine, it is a demonstration of faith, individual and corporate, that 'his blood availed for me'. We meet as a body which believes that, as one.

Have you ever considered the potential power which there is in that – ten people, twenty people, fifty, a hundred, five hundred people, not only believing in common, but thoroughly committed to what they profess?

The great social movements of history give ample illustration. Take the Chartists of the nineteenth century, for example, who joined in protest over the Electoral Reform Bill of 1832. That Bill had made changes, but not enough. It did not provide for parliamentary seats to represent the sprawling manufacturing cities where the masses lived in misery. It had not extended the right to vote to those who did not own property. So a great swell of public opinion brought the Chartist movement to birth among the working classes. It was a heterogeneous movement. Not all working men had the same education. Not all had the same pay, or the same working and living conditions. There were wide discrepancies between them. Yet, whatever their differences, there were certain beliefs which they held in common. And a slogan summarized the basic creed of all: 'One man, one vote!'

Today, we take it for granted, but our right to vote was won at a price, and we owe much to those whose common belief united them to struggle for an idea whose time had come.

As we come to this table, we come in unity of faith. However different our backgrounds, our temperaments, our interests, we are united in belief. We too have our watchword and slogan: 'Jesus is Lord'. And what power there is in that idea, when it ceases to be just a mental notion, but one to whose realization we are committed! What a revolution would take place, if a great groundswell of opinion determined to leave this table this morning, and make Jesus Lord! What a change there would be in our community and in our nation, if we decided to let him have the rule in our home lives, in our working lives, in our social lives and in political life!

Yes, we are one in faith. We say it with our lips. But the question is, will you be one of the ten, the twenty, the fifty, the hundred, who will not only say it, but say it with commitment?

3 To come to this table is to testify that we are *one in expectation.*

45

Whatever else this sacrament does, it reminds us of what that is. We celebrate the Lord's Supper because, by it, we proclaim the Lord's death. But we do it, as Paul says, 'until he come'. That is the great event which the Christian Church anticipates. It is our expectation that 'Christ is coming'!

We sing it in our Advent hymns:

> Christ is coming! let creation
> From her groans and travail cease;
> Let the glorious proclamation
> Hope restore and faith increase.
> Christ is coming! Christ is coming!
> Come, thou blessed Prince of peace.

The confidence of the church throughout the centuries, is that Christ's kingdom cannot fail, and that one day the whole universe will acknowledge him as Lord of all. That day has not yet come. 'We see', said the author of Hebrews, 'not yet all things subjected to him. But we behold him crowned with glory and honour.' No, the day has not come yet. But we can work for it. We can pray for it. And we can dedicate ourselves to working for that end.

I wonder if you have ever heard of the Minutemen? There is a monument to them at Concord in Massachusetts. During the American War of Independence, with which we began this sermon, the colonists had no regular army. But what they did have was a host of volunteers – mostly farmers and farm workers who had pledged themselves to be ready at a minute's notice, to leave whatever they were doing, to go and fight for their country. Independence had been declared, but it was not yet an actuality. And the Minutemen were prepared, if need be, to drop everything, and fight for their certain dream.

Is that not a picture of what the Church should be, and of our role as members of it? It should be a dedicated army of men and women whose one expectation, even among all our worldly affairs, is the triumph of Christ. Sensing the thrill of it, and the certainty of it, we should be like the Minutemen, ready to raise his standard, to fight for his ends, to ·ensure that his will is done wherever it can be done in the world. And we should do it because our confidence is that Christ is coming! His victory is assured! It is on the way! Ever nearer and nearer draws the time.

To come to this table is to be made conscious of our unity. It is a unity of fellowship, of faith, and of expectation. As we take the bread and wine this morning, may there be no division among us over these, and may we dedicate ourselves to them and to our Lord anew.

PRAYER

O God our Father, as we come now to the table of our Lord
    Jesus Christ,
Help us to leave behind us
All that would hinder our unity:
Our petty grievances,
Our readiness to take offence,
Our reluctance to forgive.
Grant that ours may truly be a fellowship
In which we are one in Christ
And one with all who love him.

As we come to the table,
Help us to see again what we commonly believe:
That you are our Father,
That you have shown your love for us all
In the life and death and resurrection of Jesus our Lord.
That you have called us to serve you
In the Church and in the world.
And strengthen us
In a unity of faith.

As we come to the table,
Help us to be one in expectation,
As servants who wait for their Lord:
Strong in faith,
Fervent in prayer,
Eager for service,
Determined that wherever it can be done
Your will may be done
In us and through us,

Because we know that victory is secure.
Through Jesus Christ our Lord. Amen

OUR VALUE TO GOD

Forasmuch as ye know that ye were not redeemed with corruptible things, as silver and gold . . . but with the precious blood of Christ.
1 PETER 1.18–19 (AV)

One of the most popular of television programmes, and one which commands a high audience rating, is the programme called the 'Antiques Roadshow'. It is a fascinating programme for a variety of reasons.

For one thing, it comes from different parts of the country, and often the articles presented reflect the traditional industries and skills of a region. So much so that we can experience a sense of nostalgia, when an object calls to mind for a moment a craft or skill which once thrived in an area, but now no longer survives.

It is equally fascinating to observe the expertise of those who know the antiques business, as they use their specialized knowledge to identify and classify and evaluate what is brought to them.

And it is thrilling for the viewer, when an item which was thought to be worthless and has been used for years for some mundane purpose, is valued for a fortune, or something that was bought in a junk shop or jumble sale for just a few pounds, turns out to be an article worth hundreds or even thousands.

Yet there is a moment when most of us feel a little sceptical as we watch that show, and it happens at the point when the owner of an article is asked by the expert whether he wishes to know its value. Most immediately declare an interest, but occasionally the reply is a nonchalant and embarrassed 'I'm not really too bothered'. Then we become sceptical because we suspect that in spite of the expressed disinterest, he is really quite desperate to know. And if, in truth, he is not, then we, the viewers, certainly are.

That verse from 1 Peter, like the sacrament which we celebrate this morning, speaks of a valuation. Both remind us of a valuation made by God.

48

1 One thing we learn as we watch the 'Antiques Roadshow', is that not all things are of equal value. In a far wider context, Jesus would have agreed with that.

Jesus, for example, loved the created order. He drew lessons from the farmer sowing his seed. He gloried in the loveliness of a cornfield, its golden stalks swaying in the wind. He delighted in the birds of the air, the flowers of the field, the colours of the morning and evening sky, the wind, the rain and the sun. All of them figure in his teaching.

Yet Jesus did not regard everything in the world of nature as of equal value. Looking at the wayside flowers, for example, he said to those around him 'If God so clothes the grass of the field, which today is alive and tomorrow is thrown into the oven, will he not much *more* clothe you, O ye of little faith?' That was not to say that the grass and the flowers of the field had no value before God. Jesus stated quite categorically that they had. But the 'how much *more*' asserts that humankind has an even higher value. Or, again, looking at the common sparrows, he says quite bluntly, 'Are you not of *more* value than they?' That is not to deny the value of the common sparrow in God's estimation. Indeed, Jesus says that although sparrows may be two a penny, not one of them even lands on the ground 'without your Father knowing'. But he still asserts that to God, man is of greater value. 'Are you not of *more* value than they?'

From the creation stories to the Gospels, there is the conviction that the God who looked on his work and 'saw that it was good', has a concern for the totality of his creation, a concern which he expects us to share. But there is also the conviction that, within that totality, God has a special regard for humankind.

That kind of preference is not strange to the antiques collector. He recognizes a certain value in anything that is 'antique', because it is the work of man in the past. Nevertheless, his own particular choice is for objects which stir him, which give him a sense of pleasure and to which he can relate. In the same way, the notion of the Bible is that God has a special concern for man, for not only is he God's creation, but 'made in his image'. That is to say, capable of fellowship with him and obedience to him. You and I have particular value to God because God can relate to us in that way.

2 Another thing we learn as we watch the 'Antiques Roadshow', is that a flaw can spoil the value of any object. The slightest tear in a

painting, the smallest crack in a vase, a scar or warp on a piece of wood, and its potential value is greatly reduced. Because of the flaw, it no longer enjoys the status it should have, and its ability to give the pleasure for which it was created is marred.

That is precisely what the Bible teaches about humankind. We too have a flaw. Made to bring joy to God and for fellowship with him, we have failed to realize our potential. For of our own free will we choose to live without God. We refuse to be what we were intended to be, to do what we were intended to do, to live as we were intended to live. Indeed, by our continual rejection of God, the divine image in us may be so tarnished as to be almost unrecognizable.

That does not mean that God values us any less. But he longs for us to realize the potential with which we are endowed. He yearns to enjoy that fellowship with us which, because of our flawed condition, he can no longer enjoy.

Jesus stressed the point again and again. Indeed, in St Luke's Gospel, he testifies unmistakably to the value that God still sets on us, and demonstrates in an unforgettable manner the depth of that longing in the heart of God. For there we find three incomparable stories which make the same point – the story of the lost coin, the lost sheep and the lost son. And we learn that, even in our lost condition, we are as valuable to God as a lost sheep is to the shepherd, a lost coin to its owner, and a lost son to his father. So valuable that he will spare no effort to seek and find us, and restore us with rejoicing when we are found.

It was the whole reason, in fact, for Jesus' coming. Jesus came to show that even the sinner is dear to God's heart, so dear that God will go out to seek and search for him. He came 'to seek and to save that which was lost'. And in his actions as in his teaching, he was forever trying to encourage those with whom he came in contact, to realize their potential.

That is why his judgements on people so often confound our scale of values. Like the antiques expert, who can recognize the value in objects which others fail to see – the painting bought in a junk shop for a few pounds, the box used for no higher purpose than a repository for safety pins – so he saw the value in people whom others considered worthless.

The woman taken in adultery, so far as the mob was concerned, was only fit to be disposed of. To Jesus she was fit to be given a new start. To his fellow Jews, Zacchaeus the tax collector was worthy of contempt. To Jesus he was worthy of fellowship. To Simon the Pharisee, the woman who anointed Jesus' feet with her tears, and dried them with her hair, was a woman of notorious reputation who should be shunned. To Jesus, her action spoke of a love which was beyond calculation.

The whole message of the Christian gospel is that, in spite of our flaw, God loves us and longs for our fellowship, for not even our condition can detract from his longing.

3 But the third thing we learn as we watch the 'Antiques Roadshow' is that an object which has lost its value can be restored. A damaged canvas can be repaired, a wooden panel can be replaced, a crack can be filled. And the end product is an acceptable item whose status is revived and which can give renewed pleasure to an owner. It can be done. And yet that kind of work is only undertaken if the item is highly valued by the owner, for behind any restoration work of that nature, which is highly specialized, there is always a cost.

In our text this morning, Peter is talking about our restoration and its cost. That is what the word 'redeemed' means. 'Redemption' referred to the restoration of something which one had formerly possessed, but which one subsequently had lost. So a slave, for example, could be redeemed, and thus regain his freedom, and it was done by the slave himself paying, or by someone paying on his behalf, a 'redemption' price for his liberty.

'You have been redeemed', says Peter to those who received his letter. 'The status which you had lost is restored to you. You can fulfil the purpose for which you were created. More than that, the act of restoration is the work of God. This is the value that he has placed on you.' But he also reminds them that the restoration was effected only at a tremendous cost, and in currency which is not in man's possession. 'For you were not redeemed with corruptible things like silver or gold, but with the precious blood of Christ.' He reminds them that our redemption price was nothing less than the death of Christ.

None of us will ever fully understand the mystery of the cross. All our attempts to explain what was achieved at that

> trysting place where heaven's love
> And heaven's justice meet

51

fall far short of the mark. All our theories of atonement are imperfect analogies, which miss something of its significance.

But this much we do know, that God was in Calvary; that there, by utterly holy and sacrificial and forgiving love, God was acting in Jesus to do something which we could never do for ourselves, and at a cost which we could never meet; and that the result of it is that our flaw is covered, so that we are acceptable to him.

Horatius Bonar says it so eloquently in his Communion hymn;

> Mine is the sin, but thine the righteousness,
> Mine is the guilt, but thine the cleansing blood;
> Here is my robe, my refuge and my peace –
> Thy blood, thy righteousness, O Lord my God.

Our flaw is covered, not by anything that we are, or anything that we have, or anything we have done, but by 'his blood, his righteousness'. Only because of that we are acceptable to God – 'ransomed, healed, *restored*, forgiven'.

Man created for fellowship. Man fallen from fellowship. Man restored to fellowship. That is what we are reminded of as we come to this table. That is why at this service we take a cup in our hands. In itself it, too, is something of an antique. For it was given by our Lord on the night before he went to the cross, and left as a perpetual reminder to succeeding generations of the value he sets on each one of us.

As we take it, we remember his words. 'This cup is the new covenant in my blood which was shed for many.' Thankfully we remember what our redemption cost, how dearly he loved us, and the worth he set on us. And in response, we commit ourselves in mind, heart and will to his service, by whom we 'were not redeemed with corruptible things, like silver and gold', but at the cost of his 'precious blood'.

PRAYER

Eternal and ever blessed God our Father,
We give you praise and thanks
That in love you created the world,

52

That in love you gave breath and life to mankind,
That in love you gave us the ability to respond to you.

But most of all we thank you
That when we spurned your love,
And the sin of our race grieved you,
You did not leave us in our sin,
But sent your Son to redeem us from sin and death.

Lord Jesus Christ,
We give you praise and thanks
For that great love of yours
By which you humbled yourself,
Took the form of a servant,
Were born in the likeness of men.

But most of all we thank you
That for our sake
You became obedient to death.
Even death on a cross.

Holy Spirit,
We give you thanks and praise
That here at this table
You bring these things to our remembrance
Recalling to us that they were done even for us,
And inflaming our hearts with love.

As we take the bread and wine,
So fill us with gratitude,
That we may leave this place
Strong in love and faith,
Resolute in will,
Eager for service,
And obedient to the rule of Christ.

In whose name we offer our prayer. Amen

THE ROBE

When the soldiers had crucified Jesus they took his garments and made four parts, one for each soldier . . . But his tunic was without seam, woven from top to bottom; so they said to one another, 'Let us not tear it, but cast lots for it to see whose it shall be.' JOHN 19. 23–24 (RSV)

I suppose for those soldiers who escorted Jesus to Golgotha, it was all just another day's work, albeit work of a kind which they would gladly have avoided. Bad enough to be serving in this remote corner of the empire, bad enough to have to maintain law and order among people who resented your very presence by the minute, without being detailed for this kind of duty. But in the army, orders are orders!

The Roman execution squad was usually comprised of a party of four, a centurion and three soldiers, and perhaps because of the long waiting time involved and the sickening nature of what had to be done, one of the perks for the four was the garments of the victim. That meant that the soldiers had a choice, for the ordinary Jew, in the time of Jesus, wore five articles of clothing – his sandals, a head-dress, a sash or girdle, a tunic and an outer cloak.

According to John's Gospel, their main work done, the soldiers turned their minds to their entitlement, and when each had selected a garment to keep, there was still one article left over. That remaining item was the tunic, a homespun, seamless garment, made in one piece. To have torn it in four parts would have been to destroy it, to render it quite useless to anyone. So the soldiers gambled for it beneath the cross as the victim suffered, and one of them, no doubt, congratulated himself when the dice fell in his favour, for at least he went off with some compensation for the boredom of the day.

No one knows what happened to that garment thereafter. But in any case, of what use could it have been to anyone? I mean, a man's bloodstained coat was hardly a keepsake. And what Roman would ever think of wearing the coat of a Jew? Perhaps it was sold for a few sesterces, to be spent on a soldier's night of revelry with his comrades.

Yet, whatever the fate of the garment, the very thought of it has provided inspiration for a number of writers.

If you have read Lloyd Douglas's novel *The Robe*, you'll remember that he makes the garment fall into the hands of Tribune Marcellus Gallio, the leader of the execution squad, and that, when the crucifixion is over, the soldiers have a party in the Procurator's palace.

The four are quite drunk, and in their state of intoxication, one of them tells Gallio to put the robe on, and to parade in it before the others; and while the idea is thoroughly odious to him, he yields to the taunts and the ribaldry of his comrades, and complies with their drunken demands.

Just in that moment, the full horror of the day grips him, and he falls into a mood of melancholy, precipitating what we would call a mental, or nervous breakdown. The blame for it all he puts on the robe, believing it to have some kind of magical, bewitching power, and he commands his slave to have it destroyed, an order which his slave neglects to obey.

Eventually, after a time of quiet convalescence, the day comes when he realizes that what has so haunted him is not in fact the robe. The robe has nothing to do with it. It is, after all, only a piece of cloth with no power whatsoever. No, the source of his troubled mind is the memory of that day, and the thought of an irreversible injustice meted out by the authorities to an innocent man, and one whose crucifixion he had supervised.

Resolved to know more of that man, and now taking the robe with him wherever he goes, he makes his way back to Palestine, meets up with the followers of Jesus and, inspired by their faith and their way of life, becomes a Christian himself. Finally he is condemned to death by the mad Emperor Caligula and, as he takes the steps to his own execution, he passes the robe to a slave, to be given into the possession of the disciple, Peter.

It is only a novel, of course, but a very moving one, and it is possible that Lloyd Douglas borrowed the idea of the power of the robe from a story which is told in all of the Synoptic Gospels.

There was a day, you remember, when Jesus was being crowded by people who craved his power as a healer. Among them was a woman, suffering from some kind of haemorrhage, a condition which she had borne for a long period of time, and because of which she had spent all her resources in hope of a cure. Timid and utterly desperate, and perhaps with a faith that bordered on the superstitious, she had said to herself, 'If I could only touch but the hem of his garment, then I shall be whole'. So, putting out her hand, she touched Jesus, or at least touched the hem or the tassels on his robe, and in so doing, she became the focus of Jesus' attention, and found the healing she sought.

Indeed, in addition to that story, Matthew has another, similar in content, in which he tells of the people of Gennesaret bringing their sick to Jesus, and they imploring Jesus to be allowed to touch the hem of his garment, so that by the touch, they might be healed.

These stories have inspired not only the novelist, but the hymn writers too. So John Greenleaf Whittier wrote:

> The healing of his seamless dress
> Is by our beds of pain;
> We touch him in life's throng and press
> And we are whole again.

And the evangelical hymn writer said:

> Oh, touch the hem of his garment!
> And you too shall be free;
> His love and power this very hour
> Can bring new life to thee!

Both of these stories from the Gospel demonstrate Jesus' response to faith – even imperfect faith! For the truth of the matter, of course, is that his robe in itself had no power. The power was not in his clothes but in his person. Perhaps that is why he was so anxious to discover the identity of the woman who had touched him. He would not let her go unrewarded, but neither would he let her imperfect faith go uncorrected. And the woman, for her part, after the encounter with Jesus, would not go home to speak of the power of Jesus' robe, but of the Saviour in whom she had found the power of God.

So whatever happened to the robe of Jesus is of no concern to us. As Tribune Marcellus Gallio saw in the novel, without the man who wore it, the robe had power neither to hurt nor to heal. Without

Christ it had no potency, no virtue whatsoever. It was simply a piece of cloth and nothing more.

But, just for a moment, let's suppose that Lloyd Douglas was right, and that the robe had been passed to Peter, and thence, eventually, to the Church. Can you imagine or doubt what would have happened then? It would have been preserved in some great cathedral as a holy relic. It would have been paraded before the wondering eyes of the faithful on high and holy days. It would have become, itself, an object for adoration and veneration, the hopeless focus of so many hopes and longings. Yet, devoid of the presence of Jesus, it would still be powerless.

Nevertheless, Jesus did leave something to his Church, and what he left was of infinitely greater value than a robe, for his presence is in it. That night before he went to the cross, he took bread and, breaking it, said, 'This is my body which is for you', and taking the cup he said, 'this cup is the new covenant in my blood', and he urged his men to repeat that action in his memory. This simple sacrament which we share now, in obedience to his command, is far more precious than any garment which he once wore, for it was given as a means of communion with him, as a means of realizing his presence. Is that not what Paul meant when he said, 'the cup of blessing which we bless, is it not the communion of the blood of Christ? The bread which we break, is it not the communion of the body of Christ?'

How sad, then, that in trying to explain the nature of that communion, and the manner of his presence in it, superstition has invaded the sacrament. Indeed, just as the woman in the Gospel story, and Marcellus Gallio in his deranged state, attributed to the robe powers which it could not possess, so to the bread and wine of this sacrament too have been attributed properties which they cannot have. As J. B. Phillips, describing the doctrine of transubstantiation, says in his book *Appointment with God*:

> Words charged with highest mystical meaning became words of magic. The very act of consecration had become a kind of supreme conjuring trick. The Mass had ceased to be fellowship in a deep mystery and had become the complicated performance of a priestly trick . . . a spectacle to be gaped at.

And lest any imagine that the Roman Catholic Church has had a monopoly of superstition, let it be said that in the Reformed Church too, ministers had to deal with a similar situation, for often the sacramental bread was secreted away from services for private consumption, in the belief that it had peculiar powers.

What Jesus told us to take was bread and wine. The elements are ordinary bread and wine, and so they remain. They are not miraculously changed into the physical body and blood of our Lord. Christ is not in the elements or under the elements. That is to attribute to them properties which they cannot have. There is nothing magical in what happens at the Communion table.

Nevertheless, that is not to say that there is no receiving of Christ in the sacrament, or to suggest that the elements are mere empty symbols. The bread and wine are given so that we might remember Jesus. More particularly, broken bread and *poured out* wine are given so that we might remember his death. But we cannot remember his death without also remembering that he has risen from the dead, and his promise that by his Spirit he would be with his Church, even to the end of the age.

So if the cup of blessing which we bless is the communion of the blood of Christ, and if the bread which we break is the communion of the body of Christ, then the fellowship which we have with the body and blood of Christ in the sacrament is a spiritual one. Nor is his presence any less real because it is spiritual. It is as real as the elements are to our senses. In receiving the bread and wine we receive, by faith, the reality of the living Christ in our hearts, and open our lives to the blessings and the benefits which Christ brings.

No, we do not have the robe of Jesus, and even if we did, without him it would be powerless. We do have this sacrament, on the other hand, which he deliberately left his Church as a means to communion with him in the here and now. How well Jesus knew our tendency to limit reality only to that which is apparent to the senses. So in this sacrament, the seen and the unseen, the material and the spiritual, come together, and as we take ordinary bread and wine, physical things, we receive things which are spiritual – nothing less than Christ himself.

Whittier, who was inspired by the thought of the robe, also has these words in his hymn:

> But warm, sweet, tender, even yet,
> A *present* help is he
> And faith has still its Olivet,
> And love its Galilee.

To know that is to know the experience which we call Communion, and it may be yours and mine, even now, as we come to his table.

PRAYER

O God our father,
For all the means of grace
By which we have been blessed
Through the Christian centuries,
We bless and praise you.

For the Church of your dear Son,
The living witness to his life and death and resurrection,
For the precious gift of prayer,
The very life breath of the soul,
And for your word to us
Contained in the holy scriptures,
We bless and praise you.

Especially at this table
We thank you for this sacrament,
Whereby ordinary material things
Become the means to the spiritual.

We remember the word of the Risen Christ,
'Behold, I stand at the door and knock.
If any man hear my voice
And open the door,
I will come in to him and sup with him
And he with me.'

Father,
As we take the bread and drink the wine
In this place,
May we be ready to respond to the Christ
Who is present with us,
Opening the door of our hearts
To receive him in faith,
And to be blessed by him,

As surely as were those
Who touched the hem of his garment.
And may we leave to bear witness
To the great things he has done for us.

Through Jesus Christ our Lord. Amen

IN REMEMBRANCE

Do this in remembrance of me. 1 CORINTHIANS 11.24 (RSV)

Shortly before his death, John Keats wrote a letter to his beloved, Fanny Brawne, in which he said, ' "If I should die", I said to myself, "I have left no immortal work behind me – nothing to make my friends proud of my memory." . . . If I had had time, I would have made myself remembered.'

Most of us can understand sentiments of that nature. The desire to be remembered is a very human one. Few cherish the prospect of fading into oblivion. Life itself may be fleeting and transient. 'Swift to its close ebbs out life's little day', as the hymn writer says. But most of us nourish the hope, nevertheless, that our 'little day' might have an enduring meaning and significance somewhere. We want to live on, like Keats, at least in the love and memory of our intimate friends and relatives, if not of an even wider circle.

In that the Son of God was no different from the rest of us. He wanted to be remembered too. That was why he took bread and wine in his hands, saying to his friends in the Upper Room in Jerusalem, 'Do this in remembrance of me'. And in so doing he entrusted them with a means of remembering him which succeeding generations of disciples would follow.

The sacrament of the Lord's Supper is, in fact, more than a memorial. But, at its simplest, that is its purpose, and I would like us to consider, as we come to the table now, how fitting it is to fulfil it.

1 Consider, in the first place, the *durable* nature of the memorial.

Listen, for a moment, to an old description of part of a church service;

> . . . There is then brought to the president of the brethren bread and a cup of wine mixed with water; and he taking them, offers up praise and glory to the Father of the universe, through the name of

61

the Son and the Holy Ghost, and gives thanks . . . And when the president has given thanks, and all the people have expressed their joyful assent, those who are called by us deacons give to each of those present to partake of the bread and the wine . . .

Those words were written around AD 150 by Justin Martyr, and, although the titles of the office-bearers may not be familiar to us, we immediately recognize a description of the Lord's Supper.

It is an inspiring thought, when we gather around this table, that we are forging yet another link in a chain of remembrance which has continued unbroken for almost two thousand years. Indeed, it is a singularly amazing thing that such a simple ritual has survived the changes and upheavals of the centuries, with an endurance not enjoyed by other memorials.

The Roman poet Horace, referring to the work of his pen, once said, 'My work is done, the memorial more enduring than brass'. Yet, while the words may well be true, the great language in which he wrote his odes is no longer spoken and, sadly, is now only studied by the few.

The visitor to St Paul's Cathedral in London can read, over the interior of the north door, the inscription, written in Latin, of the architect, Sir Christopher Wren: 'If you would see his monument, look around you'. But the visitor is also reminded, by many inscriptions of far more recent vintage, which appeal for support, of the decay to which such a memorial is subject, and of the cost of maintaining it intact for posterity.

The simple memorials which we erect to our own dear dead too, deteriorate in time, when neglect and the ravages of the climate combine to obliterate a once carefully worded legend. Sir Walter Scott named his novel *Old Mortality* after a man called Robert Paterson, a contemporary who earned the epithet from his determination to reverse the process by restoring the illustrious names of the Covenanters to their headstones, thus bringing 'oblivion into day'.

In contrast to our short-lived memorials, however, how imperishable the Lord's Supper has proved. In *The Communion of the Lord's Supper*, A. F. Simpson expressed it like this: 'A striking fact about the Lord's Supper is its persistence. It is as old as Christianity. We cannot but feel . . . the unmatched greatness of an act, that in its essential characteristics, is what it was when Imperial Rome was venerated as eternal.'

62

That is a remarkable consideration. Mighty empires have risen and fallen. Conquering heroes have come and gone. Yet through them, and through all the turmoil they have left in their wake, this sacrament has remained. How wise then was our Lord when he left a living memorial to be enacted by the faithful, and how trusting! It is one reason why no true follower will ever treat the matter of attendance at the sacrament lightly.

2 Consider, secondly, the *descriptive* nature of the memorial.

The purpose of any memorial, whether that of a simple stone in a country churchyard or a towering edifice like that of the Scott Memorial on Edinburgh's Princes Street, is twofold. Its function is to state who is to be remembered, and the period at which the person lived.

The Lord's Supper fulfils both. Not by any inscription on stone, but by his own words and actions committed to and repeated by the faithful, it recalls Jesus. It is done 'in remembrance of him', as the words of the Supper itself and the carving around many a Communion table remind us, while the words of the Creed, repeated at the sacrament, 'suffered under Pontius Pilate,' place him in time.

But sometimes a memorial has a third function. It sets out to relate why the name commemorated is worthy of memory, whether to a small family circle or to a whole nation.

Recently I read a memorial to Henry Hill Hickman, whose name is worthy of memory. He was born in 1800, and at twenty-one had qualified as a surgeon. Like many of his day, he was distressed at the pain of surgery. So, as a young man, he experimented in inhaling gases, hoping to find an anaesthetic, and, doubtless leaning on the work of Sir Humphrey Davy, discovered that nitrous oxide had the required effect. But he was unable to convince the medical world and, disappointed, he died at the age of thirty. It was only in 1912 that Hickman's work was recognized, and a memorial was erected describing him as 'the earliest known pioneer of anaesthesia by inhalation'.

As a memorial, this sacrament not only sets out for us who we remember, and places him at a particular point in time, but describes with a power beyond any words to express, what Jesus did that is worthy of remembrance. For the Supper is a dramatic representation of the cross. The symbols, the action and the words of the sacrament combine as a vivid reminder of Calvary, of his body broken and his blood shed, and of the costliness of that reconciling act between God and man. And when we remember, in the words of St Paul, that it was 'while we were yet sinners' that Christ died for us, then it has the power to move us to a reciprocal love and gratitude, as nothing else can.

One of the patrons of the poet Robert Burns was James, Earl of Glencairn, after whom Burns named one of his sons. Glencairn died in Falmouth at the age of forty-one, when a voyage to Lisbon failed to restore his broken health, and in a tribute of sorrow and affection Burns penned a lament which closed with these words:

> The bridegroom may forget the bride,
> Was made his wedded wife yestreen;
> The monarch may forget the crown
> That on his head an hour has been;
> The mother may forget her child
> That smiles sae sweetly on her knee;
> But I'll remember thee, Glencairn,
> And a' that thou hast done for me!'

At this table we remember Jesus. As the bread is broken and the cup is passed, we remember his suffering and death on the cross. But when we take the elements in our own hands, we realize that we who participate are ourselves the beneficiaries of his death, and we remember most of all, all that he has 'done for me'.

3 Consider, thirdly, the *dependent* nature of the memorial.

It is true, quite literally, that Jesus has placed his memorial in our hands. His command to 'do this in remembrance of him', will only be perpetuated as long as there are those who are willing to prepare it and share it. And it is a sobering thought that Jesus counts on us to keep his memorial alive.

There is a passage in Shakespeare's *Hamlet*, where the Prince of Denmark, as he lies dying, makes a plea to his friend Horatio:

> If thou didst ever hold me in thy heart,
> Absent thee from felicity awhile,
> And in this harsh world draw thy breath in pain,
> To tell my story.

That was precisely the command that Jesus gave his men on three occasions. To his friends he entrusted the good news: 'Go ye into all the world and preach the gospel'. To his friends he entrusted his testimony: 'For you shall be my witnesses, in Judaea and Samaria and to the uttermost parts of the earth'. And to his friends, in the Upper Room at Jerusalem, he entrusted this memorial of his death: 'Do this, in remembrance of me'.

Amid all the business of our lives, Jesus relies on us not to forget him. He depends on our faithfulness today, as he depended on the faithfulness of his first disciples. For his gospel, his witness, and his memorial, he has left in the hands of those who hold him in their heart.

Christina Rossetti once wrote:

> Remember me when I am gone away,
> Gone far away into the silent land.

These words could never be written of Jesus, for he is with us still by his Spirit, and by his Spirit is present at this table. But he did ask those who loved him that his death might be remembered, and that is a sacred charge entrusted to every generation of Christian people.

> According to thy gracious word,
>   In meek humility,
> This will I do, my dying Lord,
>   I will remember thee.

Yes, this we will do, because just as he counts on us, so all our hope is in him. Indeed our plea, like that of one who hung beside him on the cross, is 'Jesus, remember me'. For our faith is that, one day we who remember him now will be remembered of him.

PRAYER

Lord, we come here now
In remembrance of your death,
As you commanded.

And we thank you
For the simple means which you have appointed,
As also for those who through the centuries were obedient
And by whose faithfulness

65

This memorial has been continued
And passed on to us.

We thank you for its eloquence
To speak of things beyond bread and wine,
That they take us in thought to the place called Calvary
Where you were crucified
In an overwhelming outpouring of love
For all of humankind.

Even more, we thank you
That the elements, taken in our own hands,
Make us realize that your death
Was for us as individuals,
Utterly unworthy as we are of such a sacrifice.

We thank you for the trust
That you have shown in us,
That the charge of your gospel,
Your witness and your memorial,
You leave in our hands.

Lord, at your table this morning,
Stir up our hearts by way of our remembrance,
And so empower us by your Spirit,
That we may walk with you
Obediently and faithfully,
As long as we have life and breath,
Confident that, at the last,
We shall be remembered by you.

For your love's sake. Amen

THE KING IN HIS BEAUTY

Thine eyes shall behold the king in his beauty: they shall see the land that is very far off. ISAIAH 33.17

These were words of faith, spoken when the tide of faith was at a very low ebb. They were words of optimism and encouragement, addressed to men who had little reason to be optimistic, for Jerusalem, at the time, was on the verge of catastrophe.

It was the end of the eighth century BC, when small kingdoms, like that of Judah, were a prey to the great world powers of the day, living continually at their mercy, and when diplomatic agencies were working full out to win security with alliances.

In the year 705 BC, Sargon, the king of Assyria, the great world power, had died. So, seizing the chance to be rid of her overlord, Judah had entered an alliance, first with Babylon, then with Egypt and a host of minor states. Any security thus gained, however, was short lived. Within four years, Sennacherib, the new king of Assyria, had established himself, consolidated his position, and come for revenge on his rebellious underlings. The result was that the little kingdom of Judah was quickly overrun, so that her king had to sue for costly terms of peace, losing everything in the negotiations except Jerusalem itself.

Bad as that was, even worse was to come. For just when the calamity seemed to have run its course, Sennacherib suddenly made a new and unexpected demand – a demand for the absolute surrender of Jerusalem – and it was backed by the menacing Assyrian forces which were encamped around the city, awaiting its capitulation.

The mood within was one of despair. Food was in short supply. Special arrangement had been made for the provision of water. The people hid in terror behind the ramparts. In utter anguish, Hezekiah, the king, had covered himself in sackcloth and ashes, the garb of mourning, while his advisers were at a loss as to what guidance to offer.

67

That was when Isaiah came on the scene, whose warning on entering foreign alliances had previously been spurned. But now, in the hour of crisis, his message is one of hope. He tells Hezekiah that God will intervene to save the city, and not to accede, therefore, to the enemy's demand. 'Thine eyes shall behold the king in his beauty', he says: 'they shall see the land that is very far off.'

That was a real cry of faith. 'Zion is the Lord's', he was saying. 'Her hope is in him alone. He will not permit Assyria to violate her, for he himself will be her deliverer.' And Isaiah's prophecy was vindicated when the menacing forces of Assyria suddenly withdrew, perhaps (if the account of Herodotus is correct) through an attack of bubonic plague in their camp, and the city was delivered.

'Thine eyes shall behold the king in his beauty: they shall see the land that is very far off.' Isaiah's words had a significance not just for Hezekiah's time, but also for the future. In the immediate, they suggested that the people would see their king replace his sackcloth with his royal apparel, for the danger would be over, while they themselves, liberated from their confinement within the city walls, would be free to travel and enjoy the open country around.

But, according to the scholars, the prophecy is really a Messianic one. That is to say that it looked forward to a Golden Age, to a coming day when the kingdom would stand secure and at peace. 'You will see a king in his beauty' – in contrast, that is, to the situation of the present time, when the king is clad in mourning clothes. Moreover, in that new age the boundaries of the kingdom will be extensive, stretching far into the distance – in contrast, that is, to the undignified and reduced circumstances which it presently suffers. 'Thine eyes shall behold the king in his beauty: they shall see the land that is very far off.' Or, as the Revised Standard Version translates it, 'they will behold a land that stretches afar'.

Perhaps it seems a far cry from the beleaguered citizens of Jerusalem long ago to you and me who come now to the Lord's table. But is not Isaiah's a timeless message? And is there not that about this very service which speaks to us still of the things he prophesied?

1 This sacrament reminds us of a greater deliverance than that which Hezekiah and Jerusalem knew, for it speaks of the human predicament and our escape from it. It tells not of a kingdom, but of a world of men and women under siege. When, like the inhabitants of the

ancient city, our enemy was encamped at our door; when there was no escape from the misery and bondage of sin and death; when we were firmly in the grip of forces over which we were powerless; when there was no hand to rescue and no strong arm to save; God himself brought us deliverance, scattering our foes and putting them to flight. It happened at the place called Calvary.

And with the ending of the siege, what liberty we enjoy! Like the citizens of Zion, now able to leave the narrow walls and streets of their urban prison, and to enjoy the spaciousness of the open country-side around them, what a freedom he has won for humankind! No longer need we be bound by the restricting demands of sin. No confining gates of selfish desire need hold us in bondage. Even the constricting walls of death are no barrier to our progress. Our captivity is ended! We are free! The way is opened to new and unlimited horizons – paths of goodness and holiness and love in which we can walk freely, and lanes of service in which we are called to run.

Listen to John Masefield describe it, in his poem, *The Everlasting Mercy*, where he makes the converted drunkard, Saul Kane, say:

> I did not think, I did not strive,
> The deep peace burnt my me alive;
> The bolted door had broken in,
> I knew that I had done with sin.
> I knew that Christ had given me birth
> To brother all the souls on earth,
> And every bird and every beast
> Should share the crumbs broke at the feast.

The cross was the greatest rescue operation in human history. What we could not do for ourselves, God did for us in Jesus Christ. That is why we take the bread and wine in our hands now. They remind us of the victory won for us by the Captain of our salvation. They are the perpetual memorial of his saving act on Calvary, and of the means and the cost of our deliverance accomplished there. 'This is my body which is for you,' 'This cup is the new covenant which is shed for many, and it cost my blood.'

2 This sacrament also reminds us that God is the continual source of our strength and, therefore, our security.

69

Like the inhabitants of ancient Jerusalem, security is an issue which concerns us all, no matter the period in which we live. We want it as individuals, and we will work our fingers to the bone to find it. We want it as a nation, and we compete in the fiercest of markets to maintain it. And among the community of nations today, there is a desperate and fevered quest for security in all its forms. But is not our greatest need, as individuals, as a nation, and as a community of nations, the very thing of which Isaiah spoke – a sense of the living reality of God as the Holy one, of God as our continual strength and salvation?

When we come to the Communion table, we are acknowledging as individuals that our trust is in him. We are affirming that he, as he is known to us in Jesus Christ, is alone the source of our strength, and therefore our real security, both now and for the future.

Some time ago, a small Roman Catholic church was dedicated on the island on which I serve as a minister, and in the absence of an organist for the service, I was approached and agreed to play, reluctant only because I knew that my performance could not match the occasion. During the celebration of the Mass, the congregation sang a hymn whose words were these:

> Lord, for tomorrow and its needs, I do not pray.
> Keep me, my God, from stain of sin, just for today . . .
> Let me in season, Lord, be grave, in season gay,
> Let me be faithful to thy grace, just for today.

It seemed to me as I sat at the organ, listening to the simple wisdom of these words and watching the reverent and expectant reception of the sacrament, that our Roman Catholic friends had much to teach us about its meaning. For, while we might well disagree with their understanding of how our Lord is present at the sacrament, how often do we participate without any real awareness that the sacrament is a means of grace at all, in which Christ is really present to empower our living day by day?

That is why the writers of the Early Church compared the Lord's Supper to the 'viaticum', or the traveller's meal. The viaticum was the provision which the traveller took for the needs of his journey. It was sustenance for the road ahead. It was the source of his strength.

Or, to change the metaphor, I remember a family outing years ago when we had gone into the hills. Suddenly we came to a broad stream, and my young son held back, reluctant to cross by means of the boulders stretching over to the far bank. But when he was offered a hand to hold, and on which he knew he could rely, how nimbly he skipped across, quite untroubled by the water below.

Is that not a picture of what we are doing at the sacrament? As we take the bread and wine, we are bringing our weakness to the strength of Christ. We are putting our weak hand into his strong hand, knowing that we can rely on him. To do that is to be strengthened for life itself, and for his service and witness, and to grow in that conviction which St Paul had when he said, 'For I am sure that nothing in life or death or in all creation, can separate us from the love of God in Jesus Christ our Lord'.

3 But this sacrament is more than a memorial of our deliverance. It is more than a reminder that God is our security and our strength for the present. For the Lord's Supper is also a pledge for the future. Indeed, it is a foretaste of the prophetic word: 'Thine eyes shall behold the king in his beauty: they shall see the land that is very far off.' That is the jubilant note which rings in all the eucharistic words of the New Testament and, unless we sound it, we rob the sacrament of its full meaning.

The Lord's Supper is a 'perpetual prophecy of victory'. Listen to Jesus in the Upper Room. Luke records his words as: 'Take this, and divide it among yourselves: for I tell you, from this moment I shall drink of the fruit of the vine no more, until the time when the kingdom of God comes.' Or listen to St Paul in the words of institution: 'For, as often as you eat this bread and drink this cup, you do show the Lord's death, until he comes.'

The sacrament is a pledge, a promise for the future. It looks forward to the great consummation of all things, when, beyond the frontiers of time itself, 'we shall see the king in his beauty'. St Thomas Aquinas expressed it to perfection in his communion hymn 'Thee we adore':

> O Christ, whom now beneath a veil we see,
> May what we thirst for soon our portion be,
> There in the glory of thy dwelling-place
> To gaze on thee unveiled, and see thy face.

Just as a road going nowhere is a nonsense; or a journey without a terminus is a nonsense; or an engagement without a marriage celebration

71

is a nonsense; so this sacrament points forward to a sure consequence, to a fulfilment in the future.

And if the Lord's Supper points to the realization of the first part of the prophet's words, 'Thine eyes shall behold the king in his beauty', it does no less of the second, 'They shall see the land that is very far off'.

That may be a mistranslation, but it is what one of our former Moderators would have called 'one of the inspired mistranslations of the Authorized Version'. For the sacrament does speak of the 'land that is very far off'. Part of the great prayer which is said at every celebration says 'With angels and archangels and all the company of heaven, we bless and adore Thy glorious name'. At this table we remember our oneness, not just with our fellow-worshippers and with the whole Church on earth, but with the saints around the throne, with those whom we have loved and lost awhile, with the great and humble who followed in their day, and with whom, one day, by God's mercy, we shall be. Of these things the sacrament is a continual pledge and sign.

To come to this table, is to remember the deliverance won for us by God in Jesus Christ, and to acknowledge that he is our continual strength and source of security. But it is also to hear the ancient promise renewed, in a context far wider than Isaiah could ever have dreamed of: 'Thine eyes shall behold the king in his beauty: they shall see the land that is very far off.'

PRAYER

Lord, you are our light and our salvation. Whom shall we fear?
You are the stronghold of our lives. Of whom shall we be afraid?

Praise be to you, O God our Father,
That when we were bound as captives to sin and death,
That when there was no escape from our enemy whose grip we could not break,
That when we would have been utterly destroyed, you came to our rescue.

Praise be to you, Lord Jesus Christ,
For your great love for men and women which took you to the
   cross,
For your victory there over the forces which held us in their
   sway,
For the salvation you won for us,
And the liberty we can enjoy because of what you have done.

Praise be to you, Holy Spirit of God,
Who bring these things to our remembrance,
Who stir within us deep feelings of gratitude,
Who, even at this table, grant us a foretaste
Of the promise of eternal joy.

Gracious Lord, as we celebrate this sacrament,
Help us to see that as you have been our deliverer in the past,
So you are our strength here in the present, and our security for
   the future.
And keep us safe until that day when we shall behold you, face
   to face.

And to you, Father, Son and Holy Spirit, one God,
Be glory and praise, world without end. Amen.

EAVESDROPPING ON OURSELVES

Having loved his own who were in the world, he loved them to the end. JOHN 13.1 (RSV)

I wonder if you have ever eavesdropped on a conversation, as one who had no right to share it. I did that on an occasion, not so long ago, albeit quite accidentally and very briefly. One night, at home, I had picked up the telephone, intending to make a call. But immediately on lifting the receiver, I heard voices quite distinctly, so that, had I chosen, I could have heard everything that the callers had to say to each other.

The 'crossed line' is a fairly common experience, and if it has ever happened to you, then you are aware of the temptation it brings with it. It springs, I think, from the assumption that the parties involved are in some way invading your property. It is your telephone after all, for which you pay rental, and you feel it is part of your home. And the temptation then is to intervene, and to say something like 'Excuse me, but you happen to be on my line. Would you please ring off and allow me to use it!'

The proper response, of course, is simply to replace the receiver, quickly and quietly, hoping that neither party will notice your intrusion, and perhaps hoping too that their conversation will be brief.

If you read the thirteenth and fourteenth chapters of St John's Gospel, then you are allowed to eavesdrop on a conversation. Indeed, the evangelist is inviting us to do it, which is why he narrates the events in the first place.

The conversation, on this occasion, is not between two people. It is among a group of men, thirteen in number. The place is the Upper Room in Jerusalem. And the occasion is the Last Supper which Jesus shared with his disciples.

When you examine these chapters, you find that after the foot washing incident, there are five exchanges of conversation, and each of them is instructive as we come to this table.

74

1 The first is in chapter 13, where the one who introduces the subject is Jesus himself. 'I say to you', he says, 'that one of you will betray me!' The disciples, according to John, looked at one another, uncertain of whom he spoke. And the Synoptic Gospels tell us that all of them, even Judas, asked the question, 'Is it I?' So the first voices we hear from the Upper Room are the voices of troubled conscience.

You can imagine James and John saying to each other in muted tones, 'How could it be us? I mean we were part of the inner circle of disciples. We were with him on the Mount of Transfiguration, and when he went to heal the daughter of Jairus. At times when the other disciples were excluded, we were there. How could it possibly be us? And yet, on the other hand, this very day we've been arguing about who should be greatest! Is it just possible that we might betray him?'

Or Philip might have said to himself, 'Surely I'm not the one! I was the very first of the disciples. I was the one who followed him right at the very beginning. And yet of all his disciples, I always seem to be the background man, the man who pushes others forward, and seem to do so little myself. Maybe I'm mistaken. Could it be me?'

And I can imagine Peter saying, 'Well it's certainly not me! That day when the crowds were tailing away, and he was disappointed, and he asked us if we too wanted to leave . . . why, I was the one who said, "Lord to whom shall we go? You have the words of eternal life!" No, whoever it is, it can't be me! And yet, on the other hand, am I not the one who earned the severest rebuke that Jesus ever gave to any of us: "Get thee behind me Satan!"? And is Satan, then, so much in my heart, that I could even do a thing like this?'

The one thing that the incident makes clear, is that one can even attend a sacrament, and leave to betray Christ! And yet we doubt it. The very idea is abhorrent to us! 'Lord, I've belonged to the Church from my childhood. It can't be me!' 'Lord, I've had all the children baptized, and I'm there in the pew every Sunday of my life. It can't be me!' 'Lord, I'm a minister, I'm an elder, I'm a Sunday school teacher. It can't be me!' And yet . . . and yet . . . remember Judas!

It was the poet George Meredith who wrote the words:

> In tragic life, God wot,
> No villain need be! Passions spin the plot:
> We are betrayed by what is false within.

The betrayal of Judas is a stark reminder that none of us ever knows the mixture of good and evil in us, the strength of what is false within. So that again and again we need to ask ourselves, 'Is it I?'

2 The second exchange comes when Jesus announces to his men his imminent departure. And as it begins to dawn on them, for the first time, that Jesus really is going away, voices are raised in protest.

'But Lord, where are you going?' says Peter. Jesus says, 'Where I am going, you cannot follow now. But one day you will.' And Peter replies, 'Lord, why can I not follow you now? I will lay down my life for you!' So Peter's was the voice of protested loyalty.

Little was Peter aware of the fall that lay before him, before the dawn would break. For alone in the courtyard of the High Priest's palace, where his alone had been the courage to follow, when the flickering firelight falling on his features brought recognition as one of Jesus' friends, and accusations were made of his complicity with the accused – then came the denial, 'I know not the man'; and the third time compounded with an oath to make it more convincing. And then came the call of 'cockcrow', bringing home the Master's words, 'Before the cock crows thrice you will deny me three times!'

'Lord, I'll follow you all my days!' 'I'll never leave you!' 'I'll give you my very all.' There was a day when you and I, too, spoke words of that nature. We did it when we first embraced the faith. Or when we took our vows as first communicants. Or maybe again at some time when we were especially conscious of the hand of God on our lives.

And yet very soon we learn, as Peter did, how easy it is to follow when we are sure of Jesus' presence, and when we have the support of others. But how totally different to stand alone, in a hostile environment, when the pressure of our peers, or the crowd, is against us.

In his book *Prayers of Life*, there is a poem by Michel Quoist, which is entitled 'The Brick'. It goes like this:

The bricklayer laid a brick on the bed of cement.
Then, with a precise stroke of his trowel spread another layer
And without a by-your-leave, laid on another brick.
The foundations grew visibly,
The building rose, tall and strong, to shelter men.

I thought, Lord, of that brick buried in the darkness at the base
of the big building.
No one sees it, but it accomplishes its task, and the other bricks
need it.

Lord, what difference whether I am on the rooftop or in the foundations of your building, as long as I stand faithfully at the right place?

The story of Peter reminds us that that kind of faithfulness demands constant vigilance and a sustained relationship with God.

3 Then the third conversation in the Upper Room is between Jesus and Thomas. For, having dealt with Peter, Jesus repeats that he is going away, and he adds 'and you know the way where I am going'. But no sooner has he taken up the thread of his conversation again, when Thomas intervenes, 'But Lord, we do not know where you are going, and how can we know the way?' Jesus replies, 'I am the way, the truth and the life'.

The voice of Thomas, as always, was the voice of reason. He could not understand, and he was not prepared to pretend that he did understand. Indeed, what he said was perfectly logical. In the first place, he did not know the goal. He had no idea where Jesus was going. And if that was the case, then it followed that he could not know the way to it.

But Jesus meets Thomas at his own level. He says, 'Thomas, I know you don't understand what is happening. Nobody does! But whatever is going to take place, you have my presence. I am the way, the truth and the life.'

How often you and I, like Thomas, want a faith that supplies all the answers, which leaves nothing unexplained, and which satisfies all our doubts. And yet, as Unamuno observed, 'Faith which does not doubt, is a dead faith'. Indeed, it is also true that a faith which supplies all the answers can no longer, by definition, be a faith at all.

At any rate, to you and me too, Jesus gives, not an argument, which very rarely settles doubt anyway, but he does give us his presence. 'I am the way, the truth, and the life.'

4 The fourth conversation is between Jesus and Philip. For Jesus' word to Thomas finished with the statement, 'No man comes to the Father, but by me. If you had known me, you would have known my Father also; henceforth you know him, and have seen him!' And having just heard what Jesus had tried to say so plainly, almost incredible though his words may have sounded, Philip makes the request, 'Lord, show us the Father, and we shall be satisfied'. So that

77

Philip's was the voice of the dullard, the man who was slow to understand.

Some time ago I was attending a committee meeting, and during a report which was being presented, one committee member interrupted with a question, the answer to which was perfectly obvious, only to be berated by another member for his sheer stupidity.

Notice how gently, in contrast, Jesus deals with Philip. 'Have you been with me, Philip, for such a long time, and yet you do not know me?'

'Philip, you were my first disciple. You've shared my company, heard my teaching, seen the things that I've been doing – broken lives mended, the fallen restored – and yet you do not know me? Philip, for all that you have followed me longer than all the others, has the truth really been so slow to come to you? He that has seen me has seen the Father!'

And how many of us, like Philip, are dull and slow in our understanding? Perhaps following for all the wrong reasons. Maybe not even certain why we are following. Belonging to his fellowship, because it's what we were brought up to do, or for the sake of the company, or maybe for the position it offers. Failing utterly to comprehend the glory that is in Christ, and to realize that his right to a claim on our lives springs entirely from this, that he is the eternal truth about God.

5 And then lastly, there was one other disciple who spoke in the Upper Room. He was Judas, the son of James, otherwise known as Thaddaeus.

His contribution comes when Jesus is telling his men that, although he is going away, nevertheless he will come back. And that when he does come back, he will disclose himself to those who love him.

But Judas, the son of James, begins to quibble: 'Lord, why will you disclose yourself only to us, and not to the world?' So Judas's was the quarrelsome voice of the man who knew better.

'Surely what you should be doing', says Judas, 'is to demonstrate yourself in the most powerful manner. In that way all men and women will be compelled to follow you, and not just your disciples! What you have to do, is to take the spectacular way, and command their loyalty by force.'

But Jesus, who had been tempted in that direction right at the start of his ministry, and had rejected it again and again, because he knew that deeds of power only dazzle for the moment and then are forgotten, pointed out that the only way is the long and ponderous way of love. And so he says to Judas 'If a man love me, he will keep my words; and my Father will love him, and we will come to him, and make our abode with him'.

That is a lesson which the Church has to learn anew in every age. As Francis Thomson put it:

> There is no expeditious road
> To pack and label men for God
> And save them by the barrel-load.

You can never win men and women for the kingdom by the compulsion of force, or the compulsion of law, or the compulsion of fear, or the compulsion of the spectacular. In its time the Church has tried them all. The only force to which men will respond is the long and patient and costly force of love.

I wonder if you have ever eavesdropped on a conversation, only to discover that the subject under discussion is yourself. That is what happens in these chapters of John's Gospel. For the Judas, the Peter, the Thomas, the Philip, the Thaddaeus, are in us all.

And yet, whatever the weaknesses of these men around the table – treachery, denial, doubt, dullness and wilfulness – Jesus loved them still. 'Having loved his own which were in the world, he loved them to the end.' And as he gave them the bread and wine, weak and imperfect as they were, so, weak and imperfect as we are, we take from his hands this morning. But Jesus will not leave us weak. He assures us too, as he assured them, of his abiding presence and his strength to empower. And fortified by him, we will return to the world, as a living sacrifice of praise, eager to follow and serve him with complete obedience.

PRAYER

Lord, on the last night of your earthly life
You gathered your disciples around you,
And you broke the bread and shared the cup.

This morning we come to your table
To repeat the action
As you commanded,
And in so doing, to remember you.
But we know more than your disciples did at the time,
For the Supper was only the prelude
To what was to follow –
Your bitter anguish and suffering on the cross,
Where you laid down your life
For us and for all of humankind.

Lord, how can you forgive us,
When we, who know of your sacrifice,
Have been unfaithful to you,
Have denied you by our deeds, if not by our lips,
Have doubted your promises and purposes,
Have been slow in our understanding and following,
And have been so sure that we know a better way
Than your patient way of love?

Lord, we know that you do forgive us
When we truly repent.
But all that we do at this table
Reminds us of what our sin cost.

So save us, Lord,
From relying on 'cheap grace',
From deeds which crucify you afresh,
From imagining that we may continue in sin, for your love to
    abound.

By your presence at this table,
Cleanse and purify us from our sin,
Strengthen and confirm us for the fight against evil,
Motivate us for noble service.

And to you be the glory and the praise. Amen

ADVERTISING CHRIST'S DEATH

Pilate also wrote a title and put it on the cross; it read, 'Jesus of Nazareth, the King of the Jews'.   JOHN 19.19 (RSV)

Today we live in a world, you and I, where almost every waking moment, we are bombarded with advertisements. The advertising industry is a mammoth operation in which billions of pounds are spent every year, in which fortunes are made, and in which every possible vehicle of communication is employed.

From the pages of the daily newspaper, the glossy magazines, the radio and television sets in our homes; from billboards set in prominent places; from public transport systems; from the silver screens of the cinemas, and from letters and attractive pamphlets which are delivered to our doors, the work of the advertisers invades all our lives.

The purpose of any advertisement, of course, is to attract attention. It is quite literally to 'turn us towards' what the promoter wishes to communicate. That may be, and usually is, to go out and buy some particular product; but it may also be to advance an idea or to impart information. Sometimes, however, the aim, like that of some of the adverts which we see today, is to issue a warning. So that advertising techniques are used, for example, to promote awareness on matters of public health.

1   The superscription above the cross of Jesus was also an advertisement, albeit a very crude and rudimentary affair. Just a few words it contained, written on a piece of wood, and the purpose of the advertisement was to issue a warning.

It was the established practice of the Romans to make a condemned man carry the transverse beam of his cross to the place of execution, and a notice of the crime which he had committed was placarded for all to see. Sometimes it was tied around the neck of the criminal himself. Sometimes it was carried on a board by the soldier leading

81

the execution squad. Then, finally, at the place of crucifixion, it was nailed to the cross.

The purpose of the exercise was to attract attention. By taking the longest route to arrive at the place of punishment, so that as many as possible were made to see what was written, it was a way of saying, not only 'This is the crime which this man has committed', but also 'This is what will happen to you, if you should think of following his example!'

So the superscription or *titulus* on the cross, on this occasion, we are told, was made out in accordance with Pilate's own instructions, and finally placed above Jesus' head. And it read 'This is Jesus of Nazareth, the King of the Jews'.

The Jewish leaders, of course, objected very strongly to the words. The idea of Jesus being advertised as a king was the last thing in the world they wanted, and it has been suggested that the Roman Procurator had a double motive for writing what he did. It may be that Pilate intended, not only to issue the customary warning, but also to retaliate against those who had put him in the position of compromising his sense of justice. Again and again at the trial of Jesus, Pilate had protested, 'I can find nothing wrong in this just man'. But when he had taunted the crowd, asking them if they wanted to see their king crucified, and the crowd, in turn, appealed to Caesar, whom they hated and despised, saying 'We have no king but Caesar', Pilate, as Caesar's representative, had found himself trapped in a corner, and yielding to the pressure of public demand.

So partly, yes, to advertise a crime – Rome could not, and would not, tolerate insurrection – but also with the motive of taunting the Temple leaders, whose sheer perversity in the matter Pilate utterly despised, he made out the notice. And when they begged him to alter it, because they found it insulting and offensive, he spoke the immortal words, 'What I have written, I have written'.

2 But Pilate was not the only man who advertised the cross. Another who did it, although his motives were very different, was the apostle Paul.

Just as the priests of the heathen temples paraded the images and the symbols of their saviour gods before the eyes of their devotees; or just as a group of protesting strikers on a picket line today, placard to the passers-by, on boards and cards and banners, their affiliation and their demands – so Paul paraded the cross of Jesus. He did it in his preaching. Indeed, advertising, or portraying, the cross, was how he described his preaching.

'We preach Christ', he told the Corinthians. But even more than that, he said, 'We preach Christ crucified'. And when he wrote his letter to the church in Galatia, he said 'O foolish Galatians! Who has bewitched you? Before your very eyes, Jesus Christ was publicly portrayed as crucified.'

The word which is translated 'publicly portrayed', in Greek is the word *proegraphē*, which literally means 'placarded'. It was the word which described the posting up of public proclamations. So Paul saw Christian preaching as a placarding, or an advertising, of the cross.

That is what he did himself, and not just in Corinth or Galatia, but wherever he went. He proclaimed the cross. He advertised the cross. He paraded the cross. He gloried in the cross. 'God forbid that I should glory', he said, 'save in the cross of our Lord Jesus Christ.'

The very obvious question, I think, must be, Why did he do that? Why did he concentrate on the cross? Why this obsession with Jesus' death? I mean, why not focus his preaching on the birth of Jesus, or the life of Jesus, or the ethical teaching of Jesus? Why did Paul's preaching centre on the cross? The answer is that it was in the cross that Paul saw the supreme action of God, the fullest expression of God's love.

The fact is that the cross of Jesus always does two things. In the first place, it exposes the deadly nature of sin. When we look at the characters in the drama of the crucifixion, we see very ordinary people, just like ourselves – Judas the traitor, motivated by greed, or ambition, or perhaps by both together; Pilate, the judge, whose sense of justice was compromised to meet public demand; Caiaphas, the High Priest, who acted on what was expedient; merchants, incensed because Jesus had spoiled their takings; a coterie of friends whose loyalty failed; the thoroughly decent people who stayed away because all they wanted was peace, and who thus allowed the rule of the mob to prevail. And the cross shows what the sin of ordinary men and women, the sin of people even like ourselves, can combine to accomplish. It can allow the noblest and the best who ever lived to be crucified.

But there is another, and more positive side to the cross. For while it does expose the deadly nature of sin, it also reveals the boundless love of God. The cross was God's way of saying 'This is how much I love you, in spite of what you have done. Even if you scourge me, and spit on me, and crucify me, I will go on loving you.'

There is a story of Philip of Macedon, the father of Alexander the Great. One day it was discovered that one of his captains had been plotting against him, so that the king was urged by his advisers to have him seized and imprisoned and, finally, put to death. But Philip declined. He said 'If any part of my body were sick, would I cut it off and cast it away? Would I not rather do all that I could to heal it?' So, contrary to the advice he had been offered, he invited the treacherous captain to his palace, loading him with gifts and presents and, by so doing, shamed the man of his treason.

Paul gloried in the cross, because he saw it as the place where God, far from meting out to sinful man the punishment he deserved, so yearned for him and loved him, that he would neither cut him off nor cast him away, but instead, in a superb demonstration of his forgiving, reconciling love, poured out on humanity the riches of his grace.

Emil Brunner once wrote: 'Only at the cross does man see fully what separates him from God. Yet here alone he perceives that he is no longer separated from God.' That is why Paul concentrated on the cross. It was because he saw that there, God was at work. 'God was in Christ', he said, 'reconciling the world to himself.' 'God commends his love toward us, in that while we were yet sinners, Christ died for us.'

For Paul, the cross was the supreme manifestation of the matchless grace of God, of which he himself had known such an overwhelming experience. That is why he gloried in it and paraded and placarded and advertised it.

3 But every Christian is also called to advertise the cross.

Is that not, in fact, what Jesus asked us to do, in coming to this table? 'Take, eat', he said in giving the bread; 'this is my body which is for you. This cup is the new covenant in my blood which is shed for many.' And Paul tells us that he also said 'Do this in remembrance of me. For as often as you eat this bread and drink this cup, you do *show* the Lord's death until he come.'

Perhaps you have never thought of the Lord's Supper as an advertisement. But that, in part at least, is what it is intended to be. The words which are translated 'you do show the Lord's death' are better translated 'you proclaim the Lord's death', or 'you announce the Lord's death'. For the word used is the word which was also used to describe a herald announcing an important message, or a preacher proclaiming the gospel.

The Lord's Supper, strictly speaking, is an acted sermon, or an acted proclamation. And a proclamation in which not just the preacher, but all who participate, join together to proclaim the Lord's death.

By our presence, we advertise our own faith. By our participation, we announce that our hope of salvation rests in our crucified and risen Lord. By our sharing in the action, we hold up to view the Redeemer's death as the foundation of our faith and hope.

As we come to the table now, that is the announcement, the advertisement, that each of us is making. We make it to our fellow communicants, and to our families, and to the world at large, in the hope that they, too, may be won to the Christian faith, and to the love of Christ, who died for them also.

Dr Samuel Johnson wrote in *The Idler* of January 1759 'Promise, large promise is the soul of an advertisement'. By sharing in the sacrament, we advertise Christ's death 'until he come', because his death not only has 'promise, large promise' for ourselves, but inestimable benefits for all. And we will go from the table determined, in our daily living, to advertise him to the world.

PRAYER

Lord Jesus Christ,
With your apostle of old we glory in the cross,
For in your acceptance of the humiliation and shame,
In your endurance of the mocking and the pain,
In your compassion, shown even in the midst of your own
    suffering,
We see the depth of God's love for us all.

Now, mindful of your sacrifice,
We come to break the bread and drink the wine
And to show forth your death
As you have bidden us to do.

Lord, not just here as we gather at this table,
But in our homes, in our work,
In all our day-to-day living
Help us to lift high the cross.

Here and now
Help us to resolve
That we will leave behind the world of self and sin,
And embrace your way of sacrifice and service and forgiving
   love
In good and holy living.

So that something of your love
May be reflected through our lives,
And others may be drawn to you.

And that you, our Lord,
May rejoice over us with gladness,
And seeing the fruit of the travail of your soul,
Be satisfied. For your love's sake. Amen

FENCING THE TABLE

But let a man examine himself, and so let him eat of the bread and drink of the cup. 1 CORINTHIANS 11.28 (AV)

I wonder if you know of an old Communion custom which prevailed in Scotland for over three hundred years, called the 'fencing of the table'? It is a strange expression, but that was the name given to an address which was, at one time, delivered to communicants immediately before they came to the communion table. Originally, it was simply called the 'exhortation' but, at a later stage, it became known as 'the fencing of the table', and until the late nineteenth century, it was an important part of the Communion service.

What happened, quite simply, was this: that after the Communion sermon, or the 'action sermon' as it was then called, the minister would announce his intention to 'fence the table'. In Reformation times, it was a simple five-minute address, and there is a specimen of the exhortation in Knox's Book of Common Order. But in later times, it developed into yet another lengthy sermon. Yet whatever its form, it was a warning to communicants before they shared in the sacrament. It advised them that, while the benefits of communicating are great for those who come in a right frame of mind, so there are dangers for those who eat and drink in an unworthy manner.

And so, in 'fencing the table', the minister would read, and sometimes even expound to the people, a long catalogue of sins and vices which rendered the communicant unworthy. 'All who are thieves, and deceivers of their neighbours', he would begin. 'All who are disobedient to father or mother or Prince or Magistrate. All who are blasphemers of God's name . . .' Then, when he had completed the list, he would debar parties who were guilty of these, or any other sins which he had named, from sharing the Communion elements.

Those who are interested in sacramental customs believe that the name 'fencing the table' came from one of two sources.

It could have arisen from a practice in the Scottish law courts, known as 'fencing the court', which probably goes back for some six hundred years. When a court in Scotland was 'fenced', the ceremony was carried out by an official bearing a mace. His duty was to deliver a brief proclamation, at the opening of the court, 'defending and forbidding in His Majesty's name, anyone to trouble or molest the court'. And there was a corresponding ceremony when the court was closed. That procedure was abolished from the High Court in 1887. But it is the opinion of some, that the old Communion custom of 'fencing the table' was derived from that practice.

There is another explanation, which is almost certainly the correct one.

It comes as a surprise to many church members today to discover that until just over a century ago, the idea of communicants receiving the Communion elements in the pew was unthinkable in Scotland. From the time of the Reformation and until about 1875, such a practice was not contemplated. Indeed, it had been fiercely resisted and rejected in the mid-seventeenth century, when the proposal was first made.

For many years, in fact, the very possession of a Communion table as a fixed piece of furniture in Scotland was rare. The long and cherished practice was for communicants to share the sacrament seated around a table which was specially erected for the purpose. Such a table could seat anything from twenty-five to eighty people, and when the sermon and the 'fencing' was over, the communicants would come to it in relays, according to the number of seats around it. There they would join in a brief 'table service', which included a short address and the distribution of the elements. Then, quietly leaving the table as a psalm was sung, the next relay took their places, and another 'table service' would begin, the procedure being repeated until every communicant in the congregation had participated.

Perhaps the most surprising thing about this arrangement was that the table, in the early days, at least, was surrounded by a fence. This was no beautiful or ornate piece or furniture, but to all intents and purposes was identical to a cattle fence, with entrance and exit gates. These gates were guarded by elders. Their duty was to collect the Communion tokens as each relay of communicants came forward – possession of a token being the sign that an individual about to enter had a right to do so.

There is, in fact, an eighteenth-century Scottish painting of a Communion service in progress, which depicts the scene perfectly. It shows twenty-five communicants seated around a long Communion table and, encompassing the whole – minister, communicants and table – there is a large cattle fence, such as I have described.

Almost certainly, then, the address which was delivered immediately before coming to the table became known as the 'fencing of the table', or sometimes as the 'debars', because, just like that physical fence around the table itself, it was designed to debar from entry those who were unworthy. And the name 'fencing the table' survived as the term for that address, long after the practice of actually placing a fence around the table was discontinued.

It is easy today to ridicule these old customs, but changes in Communion practice were resented. Surprisingly perhaps, resistance was often stronger among the people than the ministers, for whom the sacramental day, with its 'action sermon', its 'fencing of the table', its address for each 'table service', and its final sermon, concluding the day, was a strain.

There is a poem, written in 1916 by the Scottish doctor and poet James Fergus, which is called 'The Parish Meenister – New Style', and of one such he writes:

> But eh, he spiles the sacrament and robs it o' its poo'er
> And gets the tables fenced an dune inside o' hauf an 'oor.

Considering the changes effected over a fairly short period of time – the disappearance of the long table, around which members had sat, listening to the 'table address' and reverently passing the elements to one another; the innovation of receiving in the pews from the hands of the elders; the discontinuing of the 'fencing' address, the 'table address' to each relay of communicants, and the final sermon – perhaps it is not surprising that many harboured resentment as cherished customs were swept away and, with their departure, a feeling that the sacrament was 'spoiled and robbed of its power'.

Yet while it is easy to laugh at our forefathers for practices strange to us today, it is worth asking the questions – What was the purpose of the 'fencing of the table'? And, perhaps of greater importance, where did they find warrant for it?

The purpose of the fencing was to preserve the purity of the Supper. It was a last-minute appeal to communicants to examine their consciences. Thus they would ensure that they came to the table prepared for what they were about to do, and in the right frame of mind. And the warrant is found in scripture, in the passage we read this morning.

Paul was writing there to the church in Corinth, where some members were making a mockery of the sacrament.

The practice in the Corinthian church was that before Communion a common meal was celebrated, and the members provided the food for it. But far from being a scene of fellowship, it proved to be totally divisive, for the Corinthian church had rich and poor members, and some of the poor were slaves. So, at this common meal, the rich gathered their friends around them, and fared very well. But the poor, in contrast, who could not afford the sumptuous provision of the wealthy, fared badly. And the result was that some, at the meal, were actually drunk, having had more than enough, while the poor, and perhaps the poor slaves especially, went hungry.

Paul was incensed at the practice, and he does not spare his indignation in the rebuke he writes to them. 'What?' he says, 'Is this the Lord's meal that you are eating? Can I commend you in this? No, I will not.' Then he reminds them of the origin of the Last Supper. 'It was on the night in which he was betrayed' that Jesus took the bread and wine, and said, 'Take, eat, this is my body which is for you. This cup is the new covenant in my blood which is shed for many.' And he tells them that, whenever the sacrament is celebrated, they are proclaiming the Lord's death. Finally he urges them, mindful of the sacred thing they are doing, to examine themselves before they come to the table, and warns them that 'whoever eats of the bread and drinks of the cup in an unworthy manner, eats and drinks judgement on himself'.

That is why our forefathers were so insistent on a self-examination. Whatever the weaknesses of the manner in which it was done, the motive for 'fencing the table' was highly honourable. It sprang from a desire to preserve the sanctity of the Supper. Its aim was that communicants should participate to their benefit. It was designed to ensure that none came to the table without serious consideration of what they were doing.

Mercifully, the Church no longer fences the table, either in word or in deed, for often the verbal 'fencing' was performed with such ferocity that its effect was to discourage people from communicating.

Parish records abound of Communion celebrations attended by hundreds, but where, after the 'fencing of the table', only a handful actually participated. Indeed one minister tells of hearing a colleague 'fencing the table' so forcibly, that he, as a hearer, felt himself debarred, and he added sardonically, 'My opinion is, he debarred himself'.

Far more true to the spirit of our Lord, is the frequently repeated story of the Free Church professor who, seeing a woman hesitate before taking the elements, said, 'Tak' it lassie, tak' it, it's for sinners'. And, in truth, that is so. The table is for sinners who are aware of their sinfulness. It was to weak and sinful men around him that Jesus gave the bread and wine at the Last Supper, and it is to those who are weak and sinful, who know their condition, their need of him, and who long for better things, that Christ still offers himself.

That, in fact, is the one sure test of our right to be at the table. Was it not Jesus who said, 'Those who are well do not need a doctor, but those who are sick. I did not come to call the righteous, but sinners'? It is the self-sufficient and the self-satisfied for whom Jesus can do nothing. It is those who come aware of their need that he can bless.

> Let not conscience make you linger,
> Nor of fitness fondly dream;
> All the fitness he requireth
> Is to feel your need of him.

Or, as John Knox put it in his 'exhortation', the forerunner to the 'fencing of the table': 'The Sacrament is a singular medicine for all poor, sick creatures, a comfortable help to weak souls . . . our Lord requireth no other worthiness on our part, but that we unfeignedly acknowledge our naughtiness and imperfection.'

We do not fence the table today. Instead, an invitation is given in the words of Jesus himself: 'Come unto me, all ye that labour and are heavy laden, and I will give you rest.' 'I am the bread of life: he that cometh to me shall never hunger; and he that believeth on me shall never thirst.' 'Blessed are they which do hunger and thirst after righteousness: for they shall be filled.'

The Lord's table is for those who know that hunger, that thirst. For all of us who come with that sense of need, his hands are outstretched to bless.

PRAYER

O God our Father,
As we come now to the table
Of our Lord Jesus Christ,
Help us to come in the right frame of mind.

Help us to come reverently
And with a hush on our spirit,
Conscious that here
We touch and handle holy things.

Help us to come humbly
And with no sense of pride,
Conscious of our weakness
And our sense of need.

Help us to come thankfully
And with hearts which are full,
Conscious of the love that surrounds this sacrament,
And all that Jesus did and suffered for us.

Help us to come expectantly
And with eager longing,
Conscious that our Lord is here
And waiting to bless.

Help us to come trustingly.
And with real faith,
Conscious that you are always faithful
And true to your promises.

Help us to come resolutely
And with determination,
Conscious that through your grace
We shall be empowered to serve you more faithfully.

Through Jesus Christ our Lord. Amen

THE EXTRAORDINARY IN THE ORDINARY

Surely the Lord is in this place; and I did not know it. GENESIS
28.16 (RSV)

*Christ Jesus . . . though he was in the form of God . . . taking the
form of a servant, being born in the likeness of men.*
PHILIPPIANS 2.6–7 (RSV)

*The cup of blessing which we bless, is it not a participation in the
blood of Christ? The bread which we break, is it not a participation
in the body of Christ?* 1 CORINTHIANS 10.16 (RSV)

'A triumph of accident and shrewd observation.' That is how one of
the most notable discoveries in the field of microbiology was
described. Every schoolchild knows the story. It was while con-
ducting research on influenza that Alexander Fleming noticed, on a
culture plate, a mould with a bacteria-free circle around it. Develop-
ing it as a liquid mould culture, he gave it the name *penicillium
notatum*, and proved its ability to arrest bacteria and bacilli. Accident
it may have been, and it certainly was a triumph, but it does seem
remarkable that what is now a valued form of medication was found
in such a prosaic place. It was the discovery of the extraordinary in
the ordinary.

The lessons this morning all speak of discoveries of that nature.

1. Jacob was on the run. Having deceived his aged father, and stolen
the blessing which belonged to his brother, Esau, he was making
good his escape from his brother's certain wrath. Preoccupied with
his flight, and before he is quite aware of it, night has fallen, and
although he is in rocky terrain, he settles to sleep under the open
canopy of heaven. Then, as he sleeps, he begins to dream, and in his
dream he sees a ladder stretching from heaven to earth, and the angels
of God ascending and descending on it. Further still, he hears the
voice of God, addressing him and promising him a glorious future,

93

and he wakens to exclaim 'Surely the Lord is in the place, and I did not know it . . . How awesome is this place! This is none other than the house of God, and this is the gate of heaven.'

That was an extraordinary discovery in a very ordinary place. An encounter with God in such prosaic surroundings was the last thing in the world he expected. And although, in one sense, it was an unsatisfactory encounter, for Jacob failed to see that he was at the bottom of that ladder and not in a position to bargain with God, the experience nevertheless assured him of God's presence.

Nor was Jacob's discovery an isolated one. In finding God in the ordinary place, he was far from alone. It happened to Moses as he tended his flock in the desert, and was drawn to the bush that burned with fire and was not consumed. It happened to the young Saul, looking for the asses of his father when, going to the prophet Samuel's house for help, he learns that God has chosen him to be the king of the nation! And it happened to Amos, herdsman and fruit picker, too. In his own words, 'I was no prophet, neither was I a prophet's son. But I was an herdsman and a gatherer of sycamore fruit. And the Lord took me from following the flock, and said, "Go and prophesy to my people Israel".' Each discovered the extraordinary in the ordinary.

Such experiences remind us that the whole earth is the House of God, and that his presence and activity is not confined to the temple or the shrine. As one who had an insight into his immensity put it:

> Whither shall I go from thy Spirit?
>   Or whither shall I flee from thy presence?
> If I ascend to heaven, thou art there!
>   If I make my bed in Sheol, thou art there!
> If I take the wings of the morning
>   and dwell in the uttermost parts of the sea,
> even there thy hand shall lead me,
>   and thy right hand shall hold me.
>   (PSALM 139.7–10, RSV)

There is a passage in Stevenson's *Misadventures of John Nicholson* when John, rather than face his father's anger at his misdemeanours, 'borrows' money from his home while his stern parent of the Disruption faith is at worship, and decides to quit Edinburgh and head for America. Taking his leave he passes St George's church on his

way, and catches the sound of the congregation singing the words of
'Ye gates lift up your heads on high'. 'To him,' says Stevenson, 'this
was like the end of all Christian observances . . . for his life was to be
cast in homeless places and with godless people.'

Perhaps that is how Jacob felt as he left his home in Beersheba.
Maybe he wondered, as he travelled, whether he had gone beyond the
limits of God's protection. Or perhaps he was as eager to escape the
judgement of God as he was his brother's anger. Who knows what
thoughts, running through his mind, might have prompted his
dream? But the fact is that at Bethel, in the lonely and deserted and
unexpected place, he was found of God.

Indeed, that encounter was to lead him to an even greater discovery,
which has been made by many another since. For who of us has not
discovered, as Jacob eventually did, that, given the chance, God can
bring good out of all the chaos we create for ourselves? Who of us has
not learned, like the dreamer on the hillside, that God can use even
our inner torment to lead us to himself? How often God uses the
unlikely place and the seemingly barren and prosaic experiences of
life as the point of encounter with us!

2. Was it not the extraordinary in the ordinary that many found in
Jesus of Nazareth?

I mean, there was nothing about his physique, so far as we know,
which pointed to anything distinctive about him. He appeared as a
man among men. Nor did his background reveal him to be 'special'.
His origins were of the humblest order. His parents were peasant
folk. He, himself, followed a very ordinary occupation. The home
town from which he embarked on his ministry was so unspectacular,
that Nathanael remarked on its plainness: 'Can any good thing come
out of Nazareth?' There was nothing whatsoever about his circumstances which set him apart. And many saw him, therefore, as a gifted
teacher and healer, but more than that they could not see. 'Is not this
the carpenter,' they asked, 'the son of Joseph?' Or, 'Is not this the
carpenter, whose mother and brothers we know?'

Nor did he possess any visible credentials which proved him different. That is what his enemies were demanding when they threw the
challenge to him, 'By what authority do you do these things?' But he
had no stamp of officialdom to establish his right. Even John the
Baptist, from his prison at Machaerus, sent messengers to him with

95

the question, 'Are you the one who is to come, or are we to look for another?' And the reply he received would have meant nothing except to the man of faith.

And yet Jesus *was* different. That was the discovery of those who were closest to him. As his life and teaching and ministry opened out to them, they saw in him the extraordinary in the ordinary. They found in him the very heart and mind and character of God. Being with him, praying with him, listening to what he said, seeing what he did, witnessing his utter faith, those who followed him were convinced of it. So that on the day when he asked them 'Whom do you say that I am?', Peter was able to reply 'You are the Christ'. And even though Peter may not have understood, at the time, all that his answer implied, it was a conviction which, far from diminishing, grew ever stronger. Especially as they followed him through the gloom of Gethsemane and Calvary, and into the brightness of the resurrection morning and the day of Pentecost.

Then, when the Gospels and Epistles were written down, the full conviction of these men as to Jesus' stature was recorded. St Paul, for example, put it this way: 'Jesus . . . though he was in the form of God, did not count equality with God a thing to be grasped, but emptied himself, taking the form of a servant, being born in the likeness of men'. The writer of Hebrews said 'He reflects the glory of God and bears the very stamp of his nature'. John wrote at the start of his Gospel 'The Word became flesh and dwelt among us', and, almost at the end of it, 'These words are written that you may believe that Jesus is the Christ, the Son of God, and that believing you may have life in his name'.

It was the conclusion of the apostles, and has been the faith of the Christian centuries that, in Jesus, we find the extraordinary in the ordinary. That is what the words of the Athanasian Creed mean: 'Truly God and truly man'. They assert that the man Jesus was nothing less than God incarnate. And the challenge which he poses afresh to you and to me and to each succeeding generation is 'Whom do you say that I am?'

3 Today we have come to celebrate the sacrament of the Lord's Supper, and it, too, speaks of the extraordinary in the ordinary. These elements which you see on the table are very ordinary things, just bread and wine. Yet in the context of this sacrament they have a

far greater significance, for they remind us of the broken body of Christ, and his blood shed. Indeed, Jesus chose them for that purpose.

That, of course, is not to say anything outwith the range of our experience, for ordinary things are often used to betoken things of greater significance. For example, some time ago, in a sale at Christie's in London, a medal was sold for the sum of £90,000 which was donated to a children's charity fund. Now £90,000 is an incredible sum to pay for a medal. I mean, a few ounces of metal and a piece of ribbon have almost no value in themselves. But the medal, in fact, was a Victoria Cross which had been awarded in 1916 to a William Leefe Robinson, for bringing down the first Zeppelin over London. That piece of metal and cloth, therefore, had acquired a significance and a value far greater than they would normally have, and the difference lay in what they represented. For they represented an act of heroism, valour and self-sacrifice, in the performance of which a man had given his life.

So with the elements on the Communion table. Very ordinary things they may be, but they represent something of far greater significance. They speak of the courage, the love, the perfect sacrifice of Christ. The broken bread and poured out wine speak of his brokenness, of the giving of himself. And the words we hear, as we take them, remind us that it was done for us. 'This is my body which is for you.' 'This cup is the new covenant in my blood, which is poured out for many.' At the Lord's table ordinary things are eloquent of something quite extraordinary.

But in the sacrament there is even more than this, for in this service we *eat* the bread and *drink* the wine, and that act too has a significance far beyond itself, for it speaks of our 'participation' in the body and blood of Christ.

What did Paul mean when he used that word? Well, participation means sharing. So in what sense do we share in the body and blood of Christ?

Paul's meaning was that as we partake of the sacrament, so we partake of the Christ who is present. Just as the food we eat becomes one with our bodies, so as we eat the bread and drink the wine, we are made one with the Christ who is present by his Spirit. And just as bread and wine nourish and sustain and invigorate the body, so at this table the believing soul is nourished and sustained and invigorated for service and holy living by the Lord himself.

William Gladstone, the Prime Minister, once wrote a fine Communion hymn, with that very idea as its theme:

> O lead my blindness by the hand,
> Lead me to Thy familiar feast.
> Not here and now to understand,
> Yet even here and now to taste
> How the Eternal Word of heaven
> On earth, in broken bread is given.

Bread and wine are such ordinary things, but they are the appointed means by which we feed our hearts on Christ by faith. Prosaic, common and ordinary they may be, but we take them now as the way to an encounter with him who is the Bread of Life, who said that those who eat of him will never hunger, and who drink of the refreshment which he gives, will never thirst again.

PRAYER

Lord, how often we miss you, because we are looking in the wrong place:
You call us to serve you in the routine and humdrum affairs of daily life.
You call us to serve you in the appeal of human need.
You call us to serve you where men and women suffer and are sad.
Help us to look for you in the ordinary places of life.

Lord, how many missed you, when you moved among men:
Some, because of their pride and self-righteousness, which blinded them to their need.
Some, because of their desire for earthly power, which prevented them from your way of love which is the greatest power of all.
Some, because their vested interests could not tolerate your truth and justice and compassion.
Help us to be among the humble poor who, aware of their poverty, see and believe.

Lord, we come to this table,
and we take common, everyday things, just bread and wine.
Help us to receive them in faith, ordinary as they are
And use them as the appointed means by which we are made
one with the Bread of Life.

And to you, with the Father and the Spirit, be glory and praise.
Amen

THE SACRAMENT OF THE SENSES

And as they were eating, he took bread . . . and said, 'Take; this is my body'. And he took a cup . . . and he said to them, 'This is my blood of the covenant, which is poured out for many.' MARK 14.22–23 (RSV)

The sacrament of the Lord's Supper has sometimes been called 'the sacrament of the tenses'. It is an apposite title, because the ordinance has a significance for the past, for the present time, and for the future. It appeals to the past as a memorial of Christ. It appeals to the present as an action to be performed in the here and now. And it also appeals to the future as a rite to be perpetuated, 'until he come'. The sacrament of the tenses is a very fitting description.

Nevertheless, I would like to suggest, today, that the Lord's Supper is not only the sacrament of the tenses. It is also the sacrament of the senses!

All that we do at this table, is done to enable us to remember Jesus, in the manner which he himself ordained. And what a stimulus to memory our senses always are! We are watching a programme on television, for example, when a picture appears on the screen of a place we once visited. And in a flash a door in our memory is opened, and we see ourselves at that scene, so that the events that happened there and the people whom we met there, flood into our minds. Or we are listening to the radio, when suddenly a tune is played, or a piece of music which we associated with some particular incident or experience. And once again, just by what we hear, our memory is stimulated, so that immediately that incident or experience is recalled to us. And so with the other senses, of touch and taste and smell – all play a part in the process of remembering.

How wise Jesus was, then, when he left this sacrament as his perpetual memorial, for the Lord's Supper appeals to all the senses.

100

Firstly, the sense of *hearing*. What is it that we *hear* when we come to this table? Well, for one thing, we hear the words of institution, and these recall to us the origin of the sacrament, and the solemn events of the night when it first began.

We hear the sound of men making their way through the streets of Jerusalem, their steps ringing out on the cobbles, and echoing from the walls of the houses. We hear them climb the steps to the Upper Room, the place which Jesus had chosen for the celebration of the Passover. And we hear the muffled exchanges as they greet one another.

We hear the conversation as the meal begins, and as we listen, we sense the sadness of the occasion, for Jesus is talking about 'going away'. We hear words about betrayal, gasps of incredulity from the men at the table, a torrent of voices loudly protesting their loyalty. And we hear the door opening and closing again as one of them takes his leave.

Then we begin to hang carefully on the words of Jesus, as he starts to speak of his impending suffering, of how this meal will be the last that they will share together, and we realize that he is speaking, not just of suffering, but of suffering to the death. We hear him telling them to eat and drink, and saying that what he is giving them will have a special significance, because it foreshadows the events which are about to take place. Then we hear them singing a hymn, and again the sound of footsteps on the stairs, as they make their way out into the darkness of the night. All this we hear, as we come to the table.

Then secondly, the sense of *sight*. What is it that we *see* when we come to this table? What we see, very obviously, is bread and wine, and we realize that that is what he passed to his men in the Upper Room. But, as we see them, we combine what we see with what we have heard, and we remember that they point to something beyond themselves. 'Take', said Jesus in passing the loaf; 'This is my body'. 'This is my blood of the covenant', he said in passing the cup, 'which is poured out for many.'

And so we leave the Upper Room and we go, in mind, to the place called Golgotha, the skull-shaped hill. And there we see the crowds, and we see the darkness, and we sense the awfulness of that place. Then, coming a little closer, we see a huddle of men, their faces twisted with raucous derision, their fists shaking with hatred. We see a squad of soldiers, playing on the ground with dice. It's all another day's work for them. And we see a group of women, their heads bowed with weeping, and their arms entwined around each other for mutual support.

Then we lift our eyes, and we see stark and bare against the threatening sky, three crosses, like giant shadows, looming out of the darkness. And our eyes are drawn to the centre one, and to the man who is dying there.

But what is it that we are looking at? Is it just another victim, dying at the hands of the Romans; another thief, perhaps, like the ones on either side of him; an insurrectionist, like so many before; another poor fool being made an example of, as only the Romans knew how? Or do we see that, in some way, although we may not fully understand, this man has done nothing wrong, and that he is there, indeed, for our benefit? Isn't this what we see?

> See from his head, his hands, his feet,
> Sorrow and love flow mingled down.
> Did e'er such love and sorrow meet
> Or thorns compose so rich a crown?

Then thirdly, the sense of *touch*. What is it that we *touch* when we come to this table? The answer, very simply, is that we touch the Communion elements. That is something which we all do. Every one of us takes a share of the bread and the wine, and as we take them in our own hands, the individualizing quality of this sacrament is brought home to us. 'This is my body which is for you' – for you who now touch. 'This is my blood of the covenant which is poured out for many' – poured out for you, who now handle.

And so we realize that while Jesus' death was for the world, it was also for us uniquely, as individuals. However unworthy we are of God's love revealed at such a price, it was for us.

> He was wounded for our transgressions,
>   he was bruised for our iniquities;
> upon him was the chastisement that made us whole,
>   and with his stripes we are healed.
>
> (ISAIAH 53.5, RSV)

Jesus knew very well the value of touch. To a group of disbelieving men he said later, 'Handle me and see' – touch me! 'For a spirit has not flesh and bones as you see that I have.' To an incredulous disciple in the Upper Room, he said 'Stretch out your finger and behold my hands' – touch me! And 'Stretch out your hand and thrust it into my side, and be not faithless, but believing'.

How often for us, as for the disciples and Thomas, it is what we can touch that convinces us of that which is almost too good to be true. The first thing the mother of a newborn infant wants to do is to hold him, to assure herself that what has happened is really true. And that grasp which is so important to the mother, is of equal importance to the child. And the husband, his heart full, arrives on the scene clutching a bunch of flowers for his wife. Not content with expressing the love and gratitude he feels, he wants to demonstrate that it is real, and he does it with visible and tangible proof, something which she can see and touch. To you and me is given at this table the tangible proof of God's love. So that, as we take the bread and wine in our hands, the symbols of Jesus' body and blood, we remember that God's love is for each of us, as individuals. Incredible as it may seem, God loves us for ourselves, and the evidence is placed in our hands, so that we may touch.

Then, fourthly, the sense of *taste*. What is it that we *taste* when we come to this table? We taste, of course, the bread and wine, the symbols which Jesus chose himself. Just ordinary bread it is, the kind we buy in the shops and eat every day of our life, and wine which is used to gladden a meal – and ordinary bread and wine it will remain.

And yet, behind these very common tastes, do we not also sense something deeper and more subtle? 'This is my body.' 'This cup is my blood of the covenant.' And so we taste the bitterness of his suffering and humiliation. We taste something of what it meant to Jesus. But we also taste sweetness – the sweetness of God's mercy and acceptance of us, the sweetness of forgiveness, the sweetness of life made new. We taste what the death of Jesus means for us, and the taste is very palatable:

> Here would I feed upon the Bread of God;
>   Here drink with thee the royal Wine of heaven;
> Here would I lay aside each earthly load;
>   Here *taste* afresh the calm of sin forgiven.

In a far deeper sense than the psalmist could ever have conceived, at this table we 'taste and see that the Lord is good'.

Then lastly, the sense of *smell*. What is it that we *smell* when we come to this table? Perhaps the immediate answer appears to be nothing. And yet, as we think of the Christ whom this sacrament brings to mind, is there not a fragrance here which is almost beyond our powers of description?

The writers of the old evangelical hymns used to apply to Jesus all the rich imagery of the Song of Solomon, and they called him the 'rose of Sharon', the 'lily of the valley', the 'fairest of ten thousand'. And isn't that really so appropriate? For in him we sense the fragrance of an utterly sinless life, as pure as the lily. And we also sense the deeper scent of his love for all mankind, represented perfectly in the pungent perfume of the rose.

There is a fragrance at this table which can pervade your life and mine. Even more, it is a fragrance which every one of us can take away with us, bearing what St Paul called the 'aroma of Christ' into all our relationships and into the routine of daily living.

In his novel *Fair Stood the Wind for France,* H. E. Bates tells the story of Franklin, a wartime Royal Air Force pilot returning from a raid, when his aircraft develops a fault and he is forced to ground in occupied France. Badly wounded in the crash landing, he makes his way to a farmhouse, and there is received, fed, provided with medical care and sheltered. One day, from his hiding place, he looks out of the open window, and after week upon week of hot summer days, he sees the rain. And the sight of the rain and the sound of it, combined with the smell of the wind, brings memories of home, and a wave of nostalgia sweeps over him. 'The rain woke in him', says Bates, 'as nothing else had woken in him, all his feelings for England. It woke in him the misery of an exile and the longing to be home.'

This sacrament, with its appeal to the senses, awakens in us as nothing else can, all our feelings for Jesus and the longing to be at one with him. With that stimulation and hearts inflamed, may we be able to leave this table with renewed dedication, saying as Peter once said, 'Lord, you know all things; you know that I love you'. And, like Peter, may we be enabled to prove it with obedient lives.

PRAYER

O God our Father,
We thank you for this sacrament,
And for all that its rich symbolism
Means to us and does for us.

For its power to stimulate our minds
To remembrance,
So that in the quietness here
Time and space are transcended,
And, in thought,
We go to that place
Outside the city wall
Where Jesus was crucified.

For its power to stimulate our hearts
To love and gratitude,
For, as we contemplate the cross,
We realize that Jesus' suffering and death
Was not only for the good of our sinful race,
But for our good as sinful individuals.
And we become deeply grateful
That your love for us
Was demonstrated through him
So willingly and at such a cost.

For its power to stimulate our wills
To long for a better quality of life,
Stirring within us an earnest desire
To live more worthily,
To serve with greater loyalty,
To follow more obediently,
And to care more earnestly.

For its power to stimulate our awareness
Of our Lord's gracious presence,
So that, influenced by his Spirit,
Our lives may be moulded to his will
And our longings for a better way
Translated into deeds.

Father,
As we come now to take the bread and wine,
May these things be.

Through Jesus Christ our Lord. Amen

DESPISING THE SACRED (A PREPARATORY SERVICE)

You say, 'How have we despised thy name?' By offering polluted food upon my altar. And you say, 'How have we polluted it?' By thinking that the Lord's table may be despised. MALACHI 1.6–7 (RSV)

> *. . . Do you despise the church of God, and humiliate those who have nothing?* 1 CORINTHIANS 11.22 (RSV)

Among the dicta of Edmund Burke, the eighteenth-century states-man and political thinker, is the saying, 'Nothing is so fatal to religion as indifference'. These words, however, would be equally true of almost every other aspect of human life – education, health, commu-nity care, leisure and entertainment, even the very welfare of the state, which was the primary concern of Burke himself! The attitude of indifference, in fact, sounds the death knell of almost every con-ceivable human endeavour. So far as religion is concerned, it might have been more meaningful, if not closer to the truth, to say that nothing is so fatal to religion as the indifference of the *religious*. That is a far more serious problem, for the indifference of the religious to the teaching and practice of their religion provides the breeding ground for self-interest, pride and hypocrisy, and all kinds of behaviour inconsistent with its aims.

The Bible brings to our notice at least two men who had to deal with that problem. Both had to face a situation in which sacred things were being treated with no small measure of indifference. Indeed, both saw a telling indication of the level of people's carelessness in the fact that the 'Lord's table' was being treated casually, and without sincerity. One was Malachi in the Old Testament, and the other St Paul in the New.

1 The prophet Malachi's situation was unenviable. Faced by an apathetic people, all the odds were stacked against him. Yet his was

the task of rallying just such a people, of reviving their faith and hope in God, and of recalling them to the worship of the Temple.

How essential that Temple had been to his nation only a few decades before! Without it, then, as a people, they could not have survived. One thing that our planners and developers today have learned, from the experience and problems of people living in post-war housing schemes, is that you cannot create a community simply by erecting a conglomeration of houses. Provision has also to be made in the form of social amenities and centres which foster a sense of belonging. So, long before Malachi's day, the prophets Haggai and Zechariah had seen a similar need for their people who, at the time, were returning from exile. The only hope of a sense of community among them, and even more, a national revival among them, lay in the restoration of the Temple. A religious base and centre was imperative. Without it Jewish society would be incoherent. So, in response to appeals, the Temple had been built, and all in the space of a few short years.

But now, around the year 460 BC, that flush of enthusiasm had disappeared, and the prevailing mood was disillusionment. It was not that the people were irreligious. They still believed in God. But they had lost their faith in him. 'Why should we serve God?' they asked themselves. 'What is the value of such service? What profit is there in it for us? Does God really care enough for us, either to help us, if we are faithful, on the one hand, or to judge and punish us for disobedience on the other?'

Nor was such a mood confined to the people. By Malachi's day, even the very priests were thinking in these terms and, influenced by the prevalent rationalism of the times, were tolerating laxity in religious practices without demur. The law was blatantly disregarded. The tithes and offerings were not being received.

One very serious indication of the state of things was the common attitude to the sacrificial system. For when it came to sacrifices, the poorest of animals were being accepted for the altar of God. Beasts which were blind or maimed were being offered. Beasts so blemished that a man would not have dreamt for a moment of offering them to the civil governor, were being brought to the Temple as sacrifices to the Lord – mere token offerings at best. And the priests who received them doubtless rationalized to themselves that a sacrifice was only a symbol in any case, and that its quality, therefore, was unimportant.

Not surprisingly and most serious of all, this defective attitude of priests and people combined had far-reaching consequences. For men were now living without principles. A general moral decay had taken place. People were dealing unscrupulously with their neighbours. The weak and the helpless were being exploited. The widow, the orphan and the stranger, who had always been the object of special compassion, were now being carelessly neglected. Any sense of community was disintegrating altogether.

Malachi saw that the root of the problem was indifference to God. So, seizing on their defective religious practices as an indication of it, he struck right at the heart of the matter, thundering against both people who gave and priests who received. Speaking for God, he says: 'You say, "how have we despised your name?" By offering polluted food upon my altar. And you say, "How have we polluted it?" By thinking that the Lord's table may be despised.'

2 Now move forward some five hundred years, and look at a group of Christian people gathered together for worship. The place is the city of Corinth, and they have come to celebrate the Lord's Supper, as we shall be doing on Sunday.

Yet clearly, from the proceedings as St Paul describes them, the celebration then was quite different from what we know today. For one thing, the meeting place was simply a private home, because at the time there were no churches. Nor is there any mention of ordained clergy to preside. But perhaps the main difference was that, in contrast to the symbolic use of bread and wine in the quantities to which we are accustomed, the sacrament was accompanied by a meal.

Yet, sacramental occasion as it was, something had gone badly wrong. The arrangement, so it seems, was either that everybody brought his own food, or that the food was bought from a common fund and then shared. But whatever the method, the meal which should have been an experience of fellowship had become one of social division. Indeed, in their gathering together, the difference between rich and poor, far from being forgotten, was actually being accentuated.

What happened in practice, was that the wealthy could provide better food, while the poor could bring little or nothing. Or, if the food was bought from a common fund, then the more opulent were able to arrive earlier than the poor, many of whom were slaves and had work to do. But, instead of waiting for the whole membership to assemble, the wealthy went ahead with their meal regardless of the others, so that when the poorer members did arrive, not only was the food gone, but some of those who had arrived at the start had taken to excess.

The whole scene then was one of extremes. On the one hand there were the better off, some of whom had had more than plenty. On the other were the poor, able to have nothing at all, and for whom the experience was one of humiliation.

When Paul got word of it, he was incensed by this behaviour, and he expressed his indignation in no uncertain terms. 'When you meet together', he told them, 'it is not the Lord's Supper that you are eating. For, in eating, each one goes ahead with his own meal, and one is hungry and another is drunk! Do you not have houses to eat and drink in? Or do you despise the church of God and humiliate those who have nothing?' Then he reminds them of the origin of the Lord's Supper and, trusting that the abuses at Corinth will never be repeated, closes by warning them not to eat or drink without 'discerning the body' – that is, without taking the fellowship of the church seriously.

3 So here we have pictures of two different groups of people who despised sacred things: the inhabitants of ancient Jerusalem who despised the altar, and the Christians at Corinth who despised the fellowship of the Lord's table.

But what was it that so angered Malachi and St Paul? What was the reason for all the fuss? Was it just the sacrilegious behaviour of the people which provoked them? No, it was the fact that men cared so little for God, of which their indifference and insincerity in religious practice was merely a symptom, that they were living without recognition of any moral authority, and therefore without moral restraint. In other words, they could treat sacred things casually, because they treated God casually, and because God meant so little to them, they could treat their fellows as of little consequence.

That is a recurring danger. Indeed, is it not the recurring story of man? We despise sacred things, treating them as a mere formality, because we fail to take God seriously, and that failure has dire social consequences. For, when we leave God out of account, we forget the sacred nature of life itself, and our estimate of man, therefore, is devalued too. So the hideous policy of apartheid denies people the right to live with the dignity of God's creatures. So the evil philosophy behind Nazism could promote and encourage the action which swept millions into the gas chambers of Europe. So the peddling of drugs for personal gain condemns hundreds of thousands to the living hell of addiction. So pure lust permits human beings to be used for the purposes of sensual gratification. Leave God out of the reckoning, and respect for man soon disappears. That is why sincerity in religious observance is so important.

In his autobiography *Adventure in Two Worlds*, A. J. Cronin, doctor and novelist, tells how, in 1938, he went to worship in a little church in the German-speaking canton of Arosa in Switzerland. He was able to follow the act of worship, but as soon as the sermon started, he was utterly lost, though he did manage to recognize two words only – *Christus* and *Führer*. Then, he says, for him, as by a breath, the church and congregation vanished:

> I saw in every land the billions of tons of armaments piled high. I saw the ever multiplying shells and guns, the stores of poisonous gas and bombs, the skies darkened by death-compelling planes. I saw children taught from their cradles to bluster and hate . . . Why in the name of reason and sweet mercy had this iniquitous bedlam come to pass? . . . There was only one reason, one basic explanation: man had forgotten God.

The issue that so angered Malachi and Paul was that 'man had forgotten God'. It wasn't so much their sacrilegious behaviour. Indifference and a casual attitude to ritual was tragic, but only because it was symptomatic of something far deeper. It was an 'outward and visible sign of an inward and spiritual disgrace'. To despise the Lord's altar or table was to despise God himself, and that had permitted them, in turn, to despise their fellows.

It was Archbishop William Temple who, speaking of the sacrament, once said 'The reality of our communion with Christ, and in him with one another, is the increase of love in our hearts. If a man goes out from Communion to love and serve men better, he has received the Real Presence . . . If he goes out as selfish as before . . . he has not received it.'

May God help us in these next few days, so to examine and prepare ourselves before we come to the table, that our Communion may be no formality, but a genuine and vital experience. For, as Jesus himself said, 'By this, all men will know that you are my disciples, if you love one another'.

PRAYER

O God our Father,
Invited to the Holy Table of our Lord,
We bow before you, conscious of our need.

As we think of the love of Jesus,
We realize the poverty of ours.
As we contemplate his goodness,
We become aware of our sinfulness.
As we consider his faithfulness and his strength to endure,
Our infidelity and weakness make us ashamed.

Father, how often we have mishandled sacred things:
Vows, once made with serious intent,
Have been broken.
Prayers for a better quality of life
Have been forgotten like a dream of the night.
Your call to us to serve you in serving our fellows
Has been abandoned in the interests of self.

Father, for our fickleness and our falsity,
And for all our failure to rise to the realization of our ideals,
Forgive us, in the name of your Son our Saviour.

Father, in these days create in us a clean heart
And renew a right spirit within us,
That as we come to the Lord's table, conscious of our need,
We may find the exceeding grace that is able to meet it.

Through Jesus Christ our Lord. Amen

THE GREAT SHOUT OF PRAISE
(COMMUNION THANKSGIVING)

To him who loves us and has freed us from our sins by his blood and made us a kingdom, priests to his God and Father, to him be glory and dominion for ever and ever. Amen. REVELATION 1.5–6
(RSV)

I have never been a football fan, but my boyhood home lay within a few miles of one of Glasgow's Old Firm football grounds. How well I remember a sound which occasionally punctuated the activities of a small boy's Saturday afternoon. It began as a low murmur coming from a distance, increased in pitch to a frenzied buzz, and finally escalated to the crescendo of a mighty roar. Even three miles away, one could tell something of the state of play, for each jubilant shout erupting in unison from the lungs of ecstatic followers on the terraces, signalled a moment of triumph as yet another goal was scored. That triumphant cheer of thousands upon thousands, which carried far over the city, was always a strangely warming sound, the noise drowning even the clanking of tram cars, the clattering hooves of carthorses on the cobbled streets, and the dull and distant thuds which constantly filled the air from the far off shipyards.

The Revelation brings to mind memories of that cheer. This verse, in chapter 1, is the low murmur, the prelude to the chorus of voices which reaches its climax in a paean of praise and a mighty shout of triumph from the lips of thousands upon thousands, in chapter 5. 'Then I looked, and I heard around the throne . . . thousands of thousands, saying with a loud voice, "Worthy is the Lamb who was slain, to receive power and wealth and wisdom and might and honour and glory and blessing!" '

Both verses express praise to Jesus. Both are eulogies in honour of the risen and exalted Christ. But I want to concentrate on this verse from the first chapter, because it tells us *why* Jesus is worthy of glory and dominion for ever and ever. It relates those things which Jesus did for us, which move not only the Church Triumphant to praise,

112

but you and me, here, in the Church Militant, to add our own voices to swell the chorus.

1 First of all, he is worthy, says the writer, because he loves us. What a simple statement that is! Nobody can ever misunderstand its meaning. It brings to mind the words of the first hymn we ever learned in childhood. 'Jesus loves me, this I know.'

But it is important to notice the tense of the verb which the writer uses here. It is the present tense. He loves us. John is talking here of the crucified, risen, and exalted Christ, and he says, not to him who *loved* us, in the past tense, but 'to him who *loves* us', right now in the present.

The real wonder of that, of course, is not just the fact of his love, wonderful though that is. The real wonder is that his is a love which was expressed in a human life and which, therefore, understands our situation, because he has been here and shared it. That is why the writer of Hebrews, also thinking of the exalted Christ, said: 'For we do not have a high priest who is unable to sympathize with our weaknesses, but one who in every respect was tempted as we are, yet without sin. Let us then with confidence draw near to the throne of grace . . .' The Jesus who loves us still, is the Jesus who took the form of a servant, shared the ordinary labour of men, and met, without immunity or protection of any kind whatsoever, the evils and injustices of his time, so that he might be one with humankind. In him, then, we can have the utmost confidence, because he has been here and identified himself with our common life.

Some time ago, Pearce Merchant, one of our Members of Parliament, tried to do something of that nature. He attempted to identify himself with the poor of our country. His aim was to live for the duration of one week on the amount he would have received, were he in receipt of social security. Then, having experienced the situation, he averred that it is possible to live in that way. Yet, whatever political motives might have prompted the experiment, it had a weakness. The flaw was that his identification with the poor was incomplete. The problem with the subsistence level provided by social security, is not in its initial effect, but in its cumulative effect. So, truly to be identified with people in that situation, one would require to begin on that level, and to continue there, having first relinquished any private resources which could be used for relief, when the ensuing misery became too great.

The wonder of the life of Jesus is that he did just that. He was 'truly man'. He came to share our human experience to the full, was identified with us completely, and knows life, therefore, as we know it, with its joys and sorrows and hopes and frustrations. So we are not to think of him now as remote and out of touch with our common humanity, or now exalted in heaven and no longer, therefore, concerned with our struggles here on earth. That is an utterly false picture and quite untrue to Jesus' nature, teaching and promises.

The love of God in Jesus, says the writer of the Revelation, never ends, but continues toward us forever. What he was, he still is. What he felt, he still feels. What he loved, he still loves.

That is why the hymn writer could sing:

> In every pang that rends the heart
> The Man of Sorrows has a part.

He has, and he does, because the Christ who loves us still, is the Christ who shared our common experience. And for that he is worthy of our praise and thanksgiving.

2 Secondly, he is worthy, says the writer, because he has freed us from our sins by his blood.

Again, the tense the writer uses is important here, for in contrast to the first phrase – 'who *loves* us', the verb *freed* is in the past tense. So what is being referred to here is a completed act, something once and for all accomplished in time. Jesus has freed us from our sins, says John, and the cost of it was his very life on the cross.

But what, in simple terms, is this freedom from sin which our mighty Liberator has won for us? It is a threefold freedom. It is a freedom, first from the pain of sin, and the pain of sin is the gnawing sense of guilt which accompanies it. Have you ever known that feeling – the longing to be free of the stain of what we have said and done, and to be clean, through and through? Shakespeare described it in *Macbeth*, when he made him say:

> What hands are here! Ha! they pluck out mine eyes.
> Will all great Neptune's ocean wash this blood
> Clean from my hand? No, this my hand will rather
> The multitudinous seas incarnadine,
> Making the green one red.

But the message of the cross is of sin forgiven, and with it freedom from the pain of our guilt:

> The cross it takes our guilt away
> And holds the fainting spirit up.
> It cheers with hope the gloomy day
> And sweetens every bitter cup.

But the cross does not only speak of freedom from the pain of sin. It speaks of freedom from the penalty of sin, which is separation from God. For the cross is the costly, reconciling act of God in Jesus, whereby we are assured of God's forgiving love and can be made 'at-one' with him. That is what the cross does as Paul saw it. 'God was in Christ reconciling the world to himself, not counting their trespasses against them.'

There is a passage in Stevenson's *Kidnapped*, where David Balfour and his friend Alan Breck have a bitter argument over Alan's gambling, and David, furious, heaps calumnies on his companion. Alan is deeply offended, and suggests that their friendship must now be terminated, as the two almost come to sword point. 'There are things said', he retorts, 'that cannot be passed over.' Immediately, David is horrified at what he has done, and he says 'I would have given the world to take back what I had said . . . No apology could cover the offence; but where an apology was vain, a mere cry for help might bring Alan back to my side. I put my pride away from me. "Alan!" I said, "if you cannae help me, I must just die here." '

In Stevenson's novel, through Alan's magnanimous nature, the plea is heeded and the friends are reconciled. But how much greater is the mighty and magnanimous love of God which streams from the cross on Calvary! For it was 'while we were yet sinners' – when things had been said and done 'that cannot be passed over', when no mere apology of ours could 'cover the offence', and before we had ever swallowed our pride and cried for help – that he took the initiative in a costly act to reconcile us to himself, making us 'at-one' with him and liberating us from the separation which our offence had caused.

And again, the freedom which Christ has won for us, is freedom from the power of sin. Almost twenty centuries of Christian witness and experience demonstrate that wonder at the cross, and what Christ suffered there on our behalf, can break the grip of sin over men

115

and women. For, responding gladly and completely, they have given themselves utterly to God in Christ and, empowered by his Spirit, have discovered moral and spiritual victory.

So, yes! For that freedom he has won for us at the tremendous cost of his life's blood – freedom from the pain, the penalty and the power of sin – he is worthy of praise.

> 'Worthy the Lamb that died', they cry,
>   'To be exalted thus';
> 'Worthy the Lamb', our lips reply,
>   'For he was slain for us.'

3 Thirdly, he is worthy, says the writer, because he has 'made us a kingdom, priests to his God and Father'.

But what do these words mean? They recall the words of God to Moses when, after the liberation from slavery in Egypt, Moses is told that Israel will be 'a kingdom of priests, and a holy nation'. That is the claim the Seer is making here for the new Israel, the Christian Church. Those whom Christ has freed will not only become a kingdom, but will be priests to his God and Father. In other words, those who respond to Christ in faith have a new status and a cause for the present, and a glorious promise for the future.

What a tremendous assurance that was to these little Christian communities in the Roman province of Asia Minor, to whom the might of Rome, under its persecuting Emperor Domitian, seemed impregnable. For they belonged to another kingdom! Persecuted, despised and dejected they might presently be, but they are citizens of that kingdom where Christ is king. And their place in that kingdom, and its ultimate victory is guaranteed.

John, the writer, himself knew something of it already. There he was, a prisoner, exiled in the stone quarries on Patmos. That was Caesar's kingdom. But he was 'in the Spirit' on the Lord's day. That was Christ's kingdom, and he knew it would prevail.

Or travel down the centuries some fifteen hundred years, to a field in Scotland where a crowd is gathered in quiet and reverent worship, and listen to John Welch, the Covenanter, preaching before celebrating the sacrament. 'We are met here this day in the name of our Lord Jesus Christ, the King and Head of His Church. These meetings, ye know, are forbidden by authority, but there is one greater than they, that commands the contrary of what they command!' For

116

John Welch, Charles the Second might be King of Scotland, and well able, with his army of redcoats, to punish and imprison and kill. But, as a minister of the gospel, his primary allegiance was to that other kingdom, whose king is Christ who rules over all!

Or listen to Dietrich Bonhoeffer, pastor and theologian, as he was led away to his execution at Flossenburg concentration camp, in 1945. 'This is the end', he said. 'For me, the beginning of life.' For Dietrich Bonhoeffer, Adolf Hitler might be Führer of Germany, backed by all the military might of the Third Reich, but, 'seeing him who is invisible', Bonhoeffer's faith was in that other kingdom whose triumph is sure.

As Christian people, we have been made citizens of that kingdom whose triumph is certain – that is our new status. For its ends we will labour in the world, offering as priests to his God and Father the sacrifice of service and intercession for our fellows, working and praying for that day when 'the kingdoms of this world will become the kingdom of our God and of his Christ, and he shall reign for ever and ever' – that is our cause. And we will do it, certain that nothing in life or death or all creation can separate us from the love of God in Jesus Christ – he is our future.

The old Scottish paraphrase sums up the content of this text so memorably:

> Thou hast redeemed us with thy blood,
> And set the pris'ner free.
> Thou mad'st us kings and priests to God
> And we shall reign with thee.

Today we have come to the Lord's table, and now we give thanks for those things of which the sacrament reminds us. What are these things? They are: the fact that he loves us; the fact that he has freed us from our sins by his life's blood; the fact that, through him, we have a status and a cause for the present, and a glorious hope for the future.

But there is only one way to give thanks, and that is by offering, in return, the kind of lives which demonstrate their gratitude in obedient living. Nothing less than a thank-offering of ourselves is enough. In the words of the prayer which was said at the table today: 'And here we offer and present to thee ourselves, our souls and our bodies, to be a reasonable, holy and living sacrifice.' That is the sacrifice of praise

and thanksgiving he is due. And to him be glory and dominion for
ever and ever. Amen.

PRAYER

Lord Jesus Christ,
You are worthy of thanksgiving.
You are deserving of praise.
And we who have remembered today
The great things you have done for us,
Would join our voices to swell the chorus
Of those who hail your triumph.

That you loved us enough to leave the courts of heaven,
That you laid aside your glory and came to share our common
    life,
That you loved sinful men and women, and love us still,
Lord Jesus, we give you praise.

That you would not leave us in our sin,
That you died to save us from its destruction,
That you have freed us from sin's pain and penalty and power,
Lord Jesus, we give you praise.

That you have made us citizens of that kingdom whose triumph
    is sure,
That you have called us to pray for it and to work for it in the
    world,
That you have set your seal on us, so that we will be with you at
    the last,
Lord Jesus, we give you praise.

Now, Lord abide with us, for it is toward evening and the day is
    far spent.
Sustain the lips which today have tasted,
And the hands which have handled holy things,
And let them be diligent in your service.

And to you be glory and dominion for ever and ever. Amen